Berta Robison

Confronting the Wind

It was in the strength of the storm that I learned to soar.

Berta

Berta Robison

Confronting the Wind

that we should no longer be children,
tossed to and fro and carried about with every wind of doctrine...
Ephesians 4:17

H1:8
PUBLISHING

Etching on Annie's sword:
μαχαιρα πνευμα ο εστι ρημα θεος
"the sword of the Spirit, which is the word of God": Ephesians 6:17.

ConfrontingtheWind@gmail.com
bertarobison.com
Soaringintheprophet.blogspot.com

Published by Hebrews 1:8 Publishing
ISBN-13: 978-0-9600799-0-2

Dedicated, with a grateful heart, to my husband, George. Without your constant companionship and biblical fluency I would not be who I am. Your skill in handling Scripture is outstanding and a gift from God. Thank you for giving me space to write this book. Iron sharpens iron…

And to Seth, Annie, and Kit, You are all deep and brilliant thinkers. Your questions were often hard and outside my paygrade. You taught me to pray in ways no one else could. I love you with all my heart. I couldn't be more proud of each one of you. You are all amazing!

And to the Holy Spirit, Thank you for Your constant companionship and for taking the things of Jesus and revealing them to me. You are the best friend anyone could have.

Contents

Book 1

Curses
Mortals' Words, Generational Curses,
Creational Curses

Section 1
Mortals' Words: Power of the Tongue

Section 2
Generational Curses: The Author

Section 3
Creational Curses: Heavens and Earth

Book 2

Demons and Christians
Limits, Aim, Influence

Preface

What we believe is our filter for everything. Our beliefs dictate how we walk before God, how we see people, sin, disease, and life. What we believe matters. What we believe about the Bible matters even more. What the Bible actually says matters most.

Everyone has theology, whether Christians or atheist. And just because we believe something does not make it true, accurate, or correct. God said that His people were destroyed because of their lack of knowledge (Hosea 4:6). How devastating when we have such an abundance of Bible study tools. People study to earn a degree, yet so many Christians don't study the Bible. Both are important, but one is vastly more important.

Book 1: Curses and Book 2: Demons and Christians have both been a subject of study for me since the late 1990s. Since George and I have moved a great deal, we have been a part of many different churches. When I first started to study these two subjects we were in a church where Christians were constantly "breaking curses" off each other and "casting demons out" of each other as their solutions to their problems. Whether it was sexual problems, financial, interpersonal, mental, or prayer problems, the answer was to break it off or cast it out. It was in the midst of this barrage of problems that the Lord opened my eyes to His truth concerning curses and demonic habitation within Christians. Jesus said, *"And you shall know the truth, and the truth shall make you free" (John 8:32).* Let us be students of the truth.

For clarity, when the words "curse," "cursing," or "cursed" are in the scriptures discussed, the Strong's reference number is provided in angle brackets (example: <0779>). The appendix provides the definitions of these words using both the Greek and Hebrew Lexicons. Sometimes a curse is inferred through the context, but the word "curse" isn't specifically in the text. Many of such scriptures are also discussed.

Acknowledgements

Two people helped me a great deal by perusing Confronting the Wind. It is with a grateful heart that I offer a special thanks to both Seth Robison, my oldest son, who is brilliant in his own right, and to Bob Merritt. Bob and Kathy have been dear friends since the early 1980s and both George and I love them dearly. Bob is exceptional in editing and knows the Bible deeply. Thank you Bob and Seth!

Special thanks to my daughter, Annie, and to my husband, George, for hiking up the rocks for the photo shoot. Annie, you are a perfect cover! Thank you so very much.

Book 1

Curses

Mortals' Words
Generational Curses
Creational Curses

I have more understanding than all my teachers,
For Your testimonies are my meditation.
Psalm 119:99

SOME TIME AGO I WALKED INTO A CHRISTIAN conference to overhear two women talking. One was telling the other how she had decided to sell a ring—a family heirloom—because she was convinced it had a curse on it. It had been passed to her from her grandmother. But now the woman, the heir, was sure it was carrying a curse. Since it was cursed, it must be sold. The Spirit of God rose up in me with such an appeal to her to come to her senses and realize who she was as a child of God. If there was indeed a curse on the ring, as a child of God, break it off in Jesus' Name!

Such is the mindset of many Christians I encounter. I would have no problem if the woman had said, "I believe God wants me to sell this ring. I don't know why, but I believe I must obey Him." The former mindset represents a powerless and misunderstood view of who we are as children of God. The latter is based on an understanding of obedience to the voice of God and a willingness to obey no matter the cost.

Another time God had given me a word of encouragement for a woman about her prayer life. This was a woman I had known for several years. At a prayer meeting, in the back of the room, one on one, I felt God nudge me this was the time He wanted to speak to her. I said something like, "The other day I felt the Lord tell me He wanted to encourage you about prayer. You are stepping into a greater area of effectiveness. He wants to tell you if you'd spend time with Him, He would give you more sensitivity to these women you are ministering to. And you would have a greater sensitivity to the Holy Spirit on how to minister to them." She got quite angry with me. She told me she'd been struggling with her prayer life throughout her whole Christian life. Now she was sure there was a curse on her to keep her from prayer. She had settled within herself to stop struggling with prayer and just wait for the curse to be broken off. She left the prayer meeting angry and in tears.

These examples, along with similar ones, are what led me to write this book. In the following pages of this book we will study curses from three perspectives: people's word curses, generational curses, and curses on creation.

Concerning people's word curses: having read some books supporting curses in Christians' lives and witnessing the destruction such beliefs produce, I found it necessary to expose these false doctrines blowing through the Church. The key question regarding mortal curses is the power of the human spoken word. Do the words spoken to or over God's people have a spiritual attachment or are words merely communication soul to soul? Meaning, are words or can words be, in a sense, like a spell with spiritual effects or attachments? Or does one's words influence another person only as that person hears the words, believes them, and then owns them? Then as they take them as their own these words then become a part of who they are changing their ideology about God, others, themselves, and the world.

Regarding generational curses: what are they and what power do they have over Christians? I know of a man, a well-known leader in a large church who has a world-wide ministry, who, out of concern for his children and their family's generational curses, had his pastor adopt him as an adult. This was well after he had his own family and his children were already grown. Consider if there really was a generational curse on their family line, then his children had already been born while still under that curse. So, **if** it was an issue of a generational curse, then the post-birth adoption by the pastor would have had zero effects on the adult children. It was too late. But he did it anyway.

Lastly, concerning curses on creation: what about the earth and creation's curse? It began in the Garden. Adam's sin having a ripple effect clearly spreads to the land, vegetation, climate, animals, the heavens, and to all of mankind. Death began to reign.

Section 1

Mortals' Words

Power of the Tongue

Your commandments make me wiser than my enemies,
For they are ever mine.
Psalm 119:9

Chapter 1

From the Mouths of Men

Words Spoken by God's People
What are the Limits?

Do THE SPOKEN WORDS OF MANKIND, believer or not, have power to kill and destroy or to give life? Is God a servant to our words or are we a mouthpiece for His? These are important questions deserving answers. So, what are the Bible's answers, for its answers will impact how we view scripture, God, others, our self, and spirits? We will examine the most prominently difficult sections of scripture for our answers to these question. For example, we will pass over Adam naming the animals (except mentioning it here), since it denotes no supernatural power. He simply named animals. We will begin with OT people: what was their understanding of the power of their words? As they spoke, why did their words have an impact and were the words themselves the source of that impact? Then we continue on into the NT's emphasis: what Jesus taught and how He ministered, Acts and the apostles, and finally, the Epistles.

Old Testament
Men of God and the Power of their Words

Noah, Ham, and Canaan: Genesis 9

Were Noah's angry words what decided Canaan's fate or was it God intervening? Furthermore, why was Canaan cursed instead of Ham? What did "his youngest son" do, as referenced in Genesis 9:24, to Noah? And whose youngest son is the scripture speaking of: was it Ham, the youngest son of Noah or Canaan, the youngest son of Ham? Theologians are divided. Ham is in the middle of almost all genealogical lists and Ham was not cursed, Canaan was. If Ham was cursed, then why did the curse flow through Canaan, his youngest, and not the rest of his children? For these reasons, I believe it was Canaan, the youngest son of Ham who did something vile to Noah. Canaan then revealed Noah's nakedness to his father, Ham, who told Shem and Japheth. With this in mind let's look at this section of scripture:

> *When Noah awoke from his wine and knew what his youngest son had done to him, 25 he said, "Cursed be Canaan; a servant of servants shall he be to his brothers." 26 He also said, "Blessed be the LORD, the God of Shem; and let Canaan be his servant. 27 May God enlarge Japheth, and let him dwell in the tents of Shem, and let Canaan be his servant.*
>
> *Genesis 9:24-27*

If Noah's words (an angry man spouting off at his grandson) directed Canaan and his offspring's lives, then that means mankind's words have creative force. Man can, thus, direct the lives of others—even nations, since Canaan was not only a man, he was also a nation (Deuteronomy 7:1-2). And if Noah's words caused Canaan's fate, then Noah's words reached into the destiny of a nation. Wouldn't that put Noah in the place of God, for it is *the Most High [who] rules in the kingdom of men, and gives it to whomever He chooses* (Daniel 4)? According to Daniel 4, God decides who receives nations, not man—not Noah. There is no other conclusion than that Noah was prophesying: foretelling, as did other patriarchs, the future of their offspring. Canaan indeed became a nation to be annihilated through Israel.

The Blessing of Isaac: Genesis 27

Isaac desired to give Esau, his first born, his blessing. However, Jacob seemingly stole Esau's blessing through intrigue. The transfer of the blessing was real: Jacob got the blessing. Esau cried with an exceedingly great and bitter cry for a blessing from his father, but Isaac said Jacob had already taken it away and Jacob would indeed be blessed. The blessing's transfer to Jacob was real and it was literal, yet, was given without Isaac's ability to rescind or annul.

From the account in Genesis it seems like Isaac has authority to command the blessings. However, the OT is always to be viewed from NT illumination. Romans 9 sheds light on this account from Genesis:

> *And not only this, but when Rebecca also had conceived by one man, even by our father Isaac 11 (for the children not yet being born, nor having done any good or evil, that the purpose of God according to election might stand, not of works but of Him who calls), 12 it was said to her, "The older shall serve the younger." 13 As it is written, "Jacob I have loved, but Esau I have hated." 14 What shall we say then? Is there unrighteousness with God? Certainly not! 15 For He says to Moses, "I will have mercy on whomever I will have mercy, and I will have compassion on whomever I will have compassion." 16 So then it is not of him who wills, nor of him who runs, but of God who shows mercy.*
>
> *Romans 9:10-16*

In Romans we see God was behind the scenes working His purposes. God ordained the older (Esau) to serve the younger (Jacob). The power to give the blessing didn't reside within Isaac. If it had, Isaac would have given the blessing to Esau. If Isaac had the power to give the blessing, would he not have had the power to rescind it? The power to root and propel the blessing rested in God alone. Romans 9 further discusses Moses, Pharaoh, and all mankind, Gentiles and Jews alike, in this same light.

Hebrews 11 illuminates Genesis 27 further: *By faith Isaac blessed Jacob and Esau concerning things to come (Hebrews 11:20). "...concerning things to come"* is a prophetic statement. Only God knows and can declare the future[1]. Isaiah 46 marries the prophetic with the nature of God—only God:

> *"Remember the former things of old, For I am God, and there is no other; I am God, and there is none like Me, 10 Declaring the end from the beginning, And from ancient times things that are not yet done, Saying, 'My counsel shall stand, And I will do all My pleasure,' 11 Calling a bird of prey from the east, The man who executes My counsel, from a far country. Indeed I have spoken it; I will also bring it to pass. I have purposed it; I will also do it."*
>
> *Isaiah 46:9-11*

When something is truly prophetic it is of necessity, then, also, truly from God. Additionally, the word "faith" always carries with it an object, meaning it always carries the assumed [in] with it. Faith is always pointing to an object of the faith. Faith means "faith in…" Faith is always attached to someone or something. For example, if I say "I have faith my house will sell today," I mean I have faith in either my own intuition, my realtor, news I've received, or that God told me it would sell today. We cannot have faith in nothing. Faith is, by nature, attached to someone or something. "I have faith my chair will hold me." My faith is [in] the structure of my chair. Many people say, "I have faith it will all end well." That phrase, even by an unbeliever, is stating a belief in God, though they don't realize it. It is stating that someone is in control of creation and is orchestrating events. (Great tool for evangelism.) So, when we see the words "by faith" in the Bible relating to God's people, we must add "in God" to "by faith," rendering, "by faith in God…" Hence Hebrews 11:20 would read: *By faith [in God] Isaac blessed Jacob and Esau concerning things to come.*

Following through in this line of thinking, when the Bible says "by faith…" we must also acknowledge that God was directly involved. Therefore: *By faith Isaac blessed Jacob and Esau concerning things to come* means: *By faith [in God] Isaac blessed Jacob and Esau, concerning things to come [for he spoke, prophesying, as directed by God.]* Furthermore, we must acknowledge that God is not in the business of being subservient to our words. (Mark 11:23 will be discussed in the next section on the NT.) God is

---

[1] Chapter 2: Last Considerations Concerning Witchcraft/Sorcery/Magic discusses witchcraft, soothsaying, and the like in detail.

interested in man hearing His words, believing Him, and speaking according to what He has said or is saying. That is the true nature of the power of man's words: words that originate with God and are in agreement with what He has said or is saying. Our faith must be [in God] lest we step over a threshold, which many others have crossed, into a doctrine of demons: a little-gods theology.

Rachel and Jacob: Genesis 31:32

Did Jacob curse Rachel with his words leading her to an untimely death? Genesis 31:32 says:

> *[Jacob speaking] With whomever you [Laban] find your gods, do not let him live. In the presence of our brethren, identify what I have of yours and take it with you." For Jacob did not know that Rachel had stolen them [the gods].*
>
> *Genesis 31:32*

Note that Jacob says, "...with whomever you [Laban] find your gods... [you Laban] do not let him live." Laban did not find the gods Rachel had stolen and therefore the statement by Jacob was null and void. His statement was Laban centric: "if you, Laban, find the gods, then you, Laban, kill the person." Jacob did not pronounce a curse on Rachel. And even if he had, would Jacob, a mortal, have the creative power in his words to cause Rachel's early death, someone he loved enough to work 14 years to marry and whom also was in the linage of Jesus Christ? If Jacob's words were binding, therefore forcing Rachel's early death, the ramifications and consequences regarding mankind's words would be horrendous. The biblical account offers no such hints that Jacob's words forced Rachel's early death. Women die in childbirth every day.

Jacob: Genesis 48-49 and Hebrews 11:21

Hebrews 11:21 is the NT's explanation of Genesis 48 regarding Jacob's blessings to Joseph's two sons: *By faith [in God] Jacob, when he was dying, blessed each of the sons of Joseph, and worshiped, leaning on the top of his staff.*

This is exactly the emphasis from Genesis:

And he [Jacob] blessed Joseph, and said: "God, before whom my fathers Abraham and Isaac walked, The God who has fed me all my life long to this day, 16 The Angel[1] who has redeemed me from all evil, Bless the lads; Let my name be named upon them, And the name of my fathers Abraham and Isaac; And let them grow into a multitude in the midst of the earth."

Genesis 48:15-16

Jacob was clearly asking God to bless the lads, for he says: *"God, before whom my fathers Abraham and Isaac walked...bless the lads (:16)."* We see faith's object is again God. Jacob spoke the blessing he had heard from God about the lads. Interestingly, Manasseh, whom Jacob claimed as his own, is mentioned in Revelation 7:6 as one of the tribes of Israel along with the other sons of Jacob and Dan is absent.

And Jacob called his sons and said, "Gather together, that I may tell you what shall befall you in the last days: 2 Gather together and hear, you sons of Jacob, And listen to Israel your father."

Genesis 49:1-2

"...that I may tell you what shall befall you in the last days" again, is a prophetic statement. We must therefore conclude it means that "God said" (Isaiah 46:9-10). Thus, we must also conclude the power to pronounce (prophesy) the destiny of the 12 tribes of Israel did not originate in Jacob, but rather in God, for only God knows the end from the beginning.

The name of Israel upon the generations to follow has indeed endured the test of time (see Genesis 48:16). Israel has withstood war, the holocaust, and the rage of her enemies' wrath desiring her complete annihilation — for God is with Israel. He told the end from the beginning.

Balaam and Balak: Numbers 22-24

Numbers is another book people use as a proof text to back up their position on the power of mankind's words. (It is irrelevant for this point

---

[1] A theophanic angel is a manifestation of God as an angel that is tangible to the human senses in the OT. In Genesis 18 and 19 we find God, the Trinity, represented as angels, men, and as the LORD.

whether or not Balaam was a true prophet.) The Bible says everyone Balaam cursed was cursed and everyone Balaam blessed was blessed. It is true, Scripture says that, but to quote this phrase without Balaam's perspective on those words distorts the truth of the text. It is forcing a view on the scriptures to make them mean something they don't. See Numbers 22-24 for the full account. For the sake of space, I briefly recount the main points of these chapters for the reader. Balak had heard about Israel's exploits and wanted Israel cursed. That Balaam's words came to pass was his reputation. Balaam's perspective about his own words are as follows:

Excerpts from Numbers 22:

> [Balak's servants said to Balaam] 17 "Therefore please come, curse <06895> this people for me." 18 Then Balaam answered and said to the servants of Balak, "Though Balak were to give me his house full of silver and gold, I could not go beyond the word of the LORD my God, to do less or more." ...38 And Balaam said to Balak, "Look, I have come to you! Now, have I any power at all to say anything? The word that God puts in my mouth, that I must speak."

Excerpts from Numbers 23:

> 8 "How shall I [Balaam] curse <05344> whom God has not cursed <06895>? And how shall I denounce whom the LORD has not denounced?"... 12 So he answered and said, "Must I [Balaam] not take heed to speak what the LORD has put in my mouth?"... 20 "Behold, I [Balaam] have received a command to bless; He has blessed, and I cannot reverse it." ... 26 So Balaam answered and said to Balak, "Did I not tell you, saying, 'All that the LORD speaks, that I must do'?"

Excerpts from Numbers 24:

> [Balaam] 9b "Blessed is he who blesses you [Israel], And cursed <0779> is he who curses <0779> you [Israel]." 12 So Balaam said to Balak, "Did I not also speak to your messengers whom you sent to me, saying, 13 'If Balak were to give me his house full of silver and gold, I could not go beyond the word of the LORD, to do good or bad of my own will. What the LORD says, that I must speak'? 14 "And now, indeed, I am going to my people. Come, I will advise you what this people will do to your people in the latter days."

God used the same wording when He spoke to Abraham in Genesis 12:3 (*I will bless those who bless you, And I will curse him who curses you*) as He did in Numbers 24:9b: (*"Blessed is he who blesses you [Israel], And cursed is he who curses you [Israel]."*) Three players are involved:

1. The person speaking the blessing or the curse,
2. Israel, the one spoken to, and
3. God the unspoken watcher/architect over it all.

This scripture does not say that the words accomplished what was spoken to Israel—the blessing or the curse. Rather, what it reveals is that the silent Architect overseeing everything watches over Israel (Psalm 121:4). He hears and sees what people say and do to His nation and rewards those people accordingly.

So we see again it wasn't the words of a man that carried power, it was God's words. It wasn't who Balaam blessed that was blessed; it was who God had blessed who was blessed. Balaam just did as he was directed by God. Even though Balaam wanted to curse Israel for money and the prestige involved (2 Peter 2:15 and Jude 1:11), he couldn't. Deuteronomy 23:5 says: *"Nevertheless the LORD your God would not listen to Balaam, but the LORD your God turned the curse into a blessing for you, because the LORD your God loves you."* Possibly referring to Numbers 22 where God had already told Balaam not to go with the Moabites. Balaam tried to twist God's arm into letting him go anyway, obviously due to the money the Moabite king had promised. God then sent the Angel of the LORD to kill Balaam, but his donkey saved his life (22:33). Numbers 23:23 sums up these scriptures very well:

> *"For there is no sorcery against Jacob, Nor any divination against Israel. It now must be said of Jacob And of Israel, 'Oh, what God has done!'"*
>
> Numbers 23:23

Joshua: Joshua 6

If taken alone, Joshua 6:26 would appear as though Joshua's words had supernatural power to perform works:

23

Then Joshua charged them at that time, saying, "Cursed be the man before the LORD who rises up and builds this city Jericho; he shall lay its foundation with his firstborn, and with his youngest he shall set up its gates."

Joshua 6:26

But when coupled with 1 Kings 16:34, the fulfillment, we find Joshua too was prophesying: *In his [Ahab's] days Hiel of Bethel built Jericho. He laid its foundation with Abiram his firstborn, and with his youngest son Segub he set up its gates, according to the word of the LORD, which He had spoken through Joshua the son of Nun.* Note that verse 34 says ... *according to the word of the LORD, which He had spoken through Joshua the son of Nun.* It began with God in Joshua and then it ends with God in 1 Kings 16. Again it is God's words that had power, not Joshua's.

Jotham: Judges 9

(Jotham speaking) *"...if then you have acted in truth and sincerity with Jerubbaal and with his house this day, then rejoice in Abimelech, and let him also rejoice in you. 20 But if not, let fire come from Abimelech and devour the men of Shechem and Beth Millo; and let fire come from the men of Shechem and from Beth Millo and devour Abimelech!" 21 And Jotham ran away and fled; and he went to Beer and dwelt there, for fear of Abimelech his brother. 22 After Abimelech had reigned over Israel three years, 23 God sent a spirit of ill will between Abimelech and the men of Shechem; and the men of Shechem dealt treacherously with Abimelech, 24 that the crime done to the seventy sons of Jerubbaal might be settled and their blood be laid on Abimelech their brother, who killed them, and on the men of Shechem, who aided him in the killing of his brothers... 56 Thus God repaid the wickedness of Abimelech, which he had done to his father by killing his seventy brothers. 57 And all the evil of the men of Shechem God returned on their own heads, and on them came the curse of Jotham the son of Jerubbaal.*

Judges 9:19-24 and 9:56-57

Verses 19-20 sound like Jotham is raging, but the rest of the account, especially verses 23-24 and 56-57, reveals he was prophesying. God sent an evil spirit and repaid Abimelech for the evil he had done (56-57). Here again verses 19-20, if isolated, sound like Jotham's curse had power, but it was, in reality, God again. God did it all.

Samuel

So Samuel grew, and the LORD was with him and let none of his words fall to the ground.

1 Samuel 3:19

1 Samuel 3:19 is an anchor scripture, meaning the entirety of Samuel's life must be viewed through the lens of this scripture; it reveals God was the One behind Samuel's words fulfilling them—every time. God let none of Samuel's words fail. Samuel was an OT prophet, which meant he was a spokesman for the Lord: *And all Israel from Dan to Beersheba knew that Samuel had been established as a prophet of the LORD* (1 Samuel 3:20). Samuel spoke God's words and God empowered those words. Therefore, even when Samuel's words appeared to have power themselves, they didn't.

Elijah and Ahab

And Elijah the Tishbite, of the inhabitants of Gilead, said to Ahab, "As the LORD God of Israel lives, before whom I stand, there shall not be dew nor rain these years, except at my word."

1 Kings 17:1

Later Elijah speaking to God concerning the duel with the prophets of Baal says: *"I have done all these things at Your word"* (1 Kings 18:36); God told Elijah to stop and start the rain. Elijah was only following the word of the LORD. Furthermore, we must again note that Elijah was an OT prophet of the Lord. Meaning Elijah's words were God's words by definition as a "prophet of the Lord."

The truth is God used and continues to use man to accomplish His works and to speak His words. He just doesn't always clearly make that distinction razor-sharp in His word. Many believers, therefore, err assuming that God's silence in some places means He has empowered people with authority to act apart from His direct involvement. God likes to use people when He acts, and yet, the distinction between God and man remains clear. Judges 7:18 says: *"When I [Gideon] blow the trumpet, I and all who are with me, then you also blow the trumpets on every side of the whole camp, and say, 'The sword of the LORD and of Gideon!'"* It's the LORD,

Gideon, and his army of 300 working together. God uses man in His plans. Man beware: don't use God.

Elisha: 2 Kings 2

Here is the question: can man—even prophets—just fling God's name around making the Name do things like magic? Elisha was a prophet and therefore the same parameters applied to him as to the other true OT prophets: prophets were God's mouthpiece, He spoke through them. And if, by chance, their words fell to the ground, the prophet was to be put to death.

> Then the men of the city said to Elisha, "Please notice, the situation of this city is pleasant, as my lord sees; but the water is bad, and the ground barren." 20 And he said, "Bring me a new bowl, and put salt in it." So they brought it to him. 21 Then he went out to the source of the water, and cast in the salt there, and said, "Thus says the LORD: 'I have healed this water; from it there shall be no more death or barrenness.'" 22 So the water remains healed to this day, according to the word of Elisha which he spoke. 23 Then he went up from there to Bethel; and as he was going up the road, some youths came from the city and mocked him, and said to him, "Go up, you baldhead! Go up, you baldhead!" 24 So he turned around and looked at them, and pronounced a curse <07043> on them in the name of the LORD. And two female bears came out of the woods and mauled forty-two of the youths.
>
> *2 Kings 2:19-24*

The lads were notably defiant, which according to the Law carried the death penalty (Deuteronomy 21:18-21). They were likely mocking Elijah's ascension in the chariot when they said to Elisha: *"Go up, you baldhead; go up, you baldhead!"* (:23). The lads were not mocking Elisha, they were mocking God, since God had done the works through Elisha and had taken Elijah up. The lads' words didn't bind Elisha. In fact, their words had consequences, consequences upon themselves. Preceding the story of the lads, God, through Elisha, had just healed water in Jericho. Verse 22 sounds as though Elisha's own words had resident power to heal the water, but verse 21 reveals Elisha prophesied according to the word of the LORD. In light of healing the water, let's look again at verses 23-24. Elisha pronounced the curse in the name of the LORD and then the bears came and tore up the lads. The lads didn't die immediately when the curse was pronounced; bears came to carry out the curse. That God would send bears to kill 42 lads is likely very uncomfortable for many readers. It seems so severe even when viewed through the lens of the OT law regarding defiant children. Such tension in our understanding reveals we must allow God to adjust our thinking, and thus see the account from His perspective.

Eliphaz: An Exercise in Exegesis: Job 22

"Decree a thing and it will be established for you" has become the emphasis of many Charismatic ministries. Since I first wrote this study I have seen entire conferences devoted to decreeing and declaring. To whom are they decreeing and declaring? That is a good question. For example, let's say I need money to pay unexpected bills. If I believe there is creative power in my declaration and decree, then my actions will be to declare and decree into the heavens or into the atmosphere or to the devil or … to God. I would say, "Release money to me. I command that all my needs are met, in Jesus Name, for He shall supply all my needs according to His riches in glory." Now, of course, there are a great number of scriptures I can quote in my decree and declaration. But, is this the biblical pattern—to speak into the atmosphere? Is this what Jesus did? The apostles? If, however, my paradigm is that God is the keeper of all my answers, the One who hears all my prayers, and who meets all my needs, then I will, instead of declaring and decreeing, simply ask.

In a meeting I attended, a leader's message was on decreeing and declaring. The point the leader was making was that we can decree a thing as the church or as an individual and it will be established for us. So, in the meeting people decreed things they wanted done. Maybe even things God wanted done? Consider if it is true that we can declare/decree a thing and it will be established, then something or someone is establishing it—for **it will be** established **for you**. Meaning again, there is a silent agent. We must conclude therefore that the silent agent is either God, the words themselves, man's own resident supernatural power, some unseen unmentioned force, or the devil. Who or what is, in reality, empowering the words?

Think about it...

Getting back to the meeting... I already had reservations about declaring and decreeing things and the power of people's words, so the sermon did not set well with me. I went home and looked in the Bible for: *"Decree a thing and it will be established for you."* There it is in Job 22:28:

> *"You will also decree a thing, and it will be established for you; And light will shine on your ways."*
>
> (Job 22:28 NASB)

...spoken by Eliphaz the Temanite... oops... Let's look at God's opinion of Eliphaz. God said to Eliphaz: *It came about after the LORD had spoken these words to Job, that the LORD said to Eliphaz the Temanite, "My wrath is kindled against you and against your two friends, because you have not spoken of Me what is right as My servant Job has"* (Job 42:7 NASB). Therefore, to use Job 22:28 as it is often used, to promote declarations and decrees, is completely against sound Biblical exegesis. We cannot pull from Eliphaz's words to establish a doctrinal position any more than we could Satan's words. For example, why is it that we never see cards or pictures with: *"Therefore, if You will worship before me, all will be yours"*? Because the source was Satan. He said this when tempting Jesus. We cannot build upon Eliphaz's words any more than we can Satan's. Both do not speak according to what is right.

The New Testament
The Gospels

Jesus' Words

The other day an acquaintance posted the following on a social media website: "?? What would happen if we walked the streets of our city, just declaring forgiveness over the people (not to people), their businesses, [and] their history?" This person has many followers who concurred with his philosophical paradigm in their comments. Many said they were already walking their streets proclaiming things over their neighbors, streets, and businesses (not to people). The word "over" verses "to" reveals the philosophy. Did Jesus do this? Did the apostles? When Jesus spoke: *"O Jerusalem, Jerusalem, the one who kills the prophets and stones those who are sent to her! How often I wanted to gather your children together, as a hen gathers her brood under her wings, but you were not willing!" (Luke 13:34),* He was speaking directly to the Pharisees. This quote begins in Luke 13:32: *...And He [Jesus] said to them [the Pharisees]...* Jesus was speaking to the Pharisees—the religious rulers in Jerusalem—not over the city itself.

Similarly, when Jonah went through Nineveh, he preached repentance to people. He did not speak into the air expecting his words to sow seeds that would change people lives without people hearing them. We don't impregnate the atmosphere, as some teach.

Something to ponder: If mankind's words have power to create and to destroy or to work in a way that is not just mouth to ear communication, then how does it all work? Are there spirits involved? Are man's words spirit and life? Who is man then, and how does he differ from God? The God/man line gets confused and blurred often, we must not get it blurred or confused. This line must be completely fixed in our understanding, theology, doctrine, and practice. God is God and we are not. We must not get confused—He alone is God. If we believe our words have creative power apart from what God is saying, we stagger into very dangerous territory—a territory into which someone else has strayed. Someone else said he'd be like the Most High; someone we do not want to be like!

This is the question: Who are we now that Christ lives in us? Is there residential power that we can wield at will or is it always the Person of the Holy Spirit that we are dealing with? Are we a new breed of a merged God-man, with resident God-like power within us? Or are we rather a new creation, born of the Spirit and our sufficiency is of God? Thus, forcing us to always rely on Him to move through us. Furthermore, what did God mean when He said: *"...you will receive power when the Holy Spirit has come upon you" (Acts 1:8)*?

Following are excerpts from a thread on my social media page, which I posted after hearing a message from Romans 4:17. It exposes misunderstandings people have on the power of man's words and how easily we get off track when we take scriptures out of context:

Straight Talk with the Preacher—

Dear Mr. Preacher,
I enjoyed your message and God even spoke to me through you today. However, I have a beef with something you said. You said we people need to call things that are not as though they are. This scripture reference is from Romans 4:17. The background is Paul hashing out the justification we have through grace because of Jesus Christ—apart from works. It is in this context of Paul saying that it is God Who has done all this: [the] *"God, who gives life to the dead and calls those things which do not exist as though they did..." (Romans 4:17).*

See, Mr. Preacher, it is God who gives life to the dead. It is God who calls things that are not as though they are. This is referring back to creation. God spoke into nothing and created everything by His Word. It is God's Word that has creative power, Mr. Preacher, not men's—not yours, not mine—God's. Man does not speak to create. God alone possesses that power. Let us not fall again to that lie from the pit of hell. We are not little gods.

Sincerely,
Berta

• BK: So... Jesus healed the sick, was translated from here to there, and even raised the dead. That being said, what do we do with Jesus saying, *"You will do greater things than these" (John 14:12)* to us? Just curious as to your take on that.

• Me: We are His servants and do as we are told. Even Jesus only did what He saw and said what He heard from the Father. Though He being the exact representation of the Father — God incarnate — He lived submitted to His will and His voice. There is a fine line between operating under His authority and commanding things through prophetic revelation/anointing verses the attitude of "I am a Christian indwelt with the Holy Spirit therefore I have authority to..."

Philippians 2 puts it this way:

Let this mind be in you which was also in Christ Jesus, 6 who, being in the form of God, did not consider it robbery to be equal with God, 7 but made Himself of no reputation, taking the form of a bondservant, and coming in the likeness of men. 8 And being found in appearance as a man, He humbled Himself and became obedient to the point of death, even the death of the cross.

Philippians 2:5-8

Furthermore, let's look at what you said in the context where Jesus spoke it.

From John 14:

"Most assuredly, I say to you, he who believes in Me, the works that I do he will do also; and greater works than these he will do, because I go to My Father. 13 And whatever you ask in My name, that I will do, that the Father may be glorified in the Son. 14 If you ask anything in My name, I will do it."

John 14:12-14

Jesus, in this whole section of John, is talking about the Holy Spirit coming and His ministry to us. Here, specifically surrounding "greater works" is the context of Jesus leaving, the Holy Spirit coming, and us asking in the Father in Jesus' Name and *"I will do it."* See it isn't even us doing the doing. It is us asking and Him doing the doing.

•JK: *"For assuredly, I say to you, whoever says to this mountain, 'Be removed and be cast into the sea,' and does not doubt in his heart, but believes that those things he says will be done, he will have whatever he says"(Mark 11:23).*

•Me: Hi JK, It is all about context. Remember Satan is a master at taking scripture out of context. So much can be understood by just looking at the origin. This scripture you quoted, JK, in context, is surrounded by Jesus talking about faith in God and prayer. So the context is FAITH and the object is IN GOD. Not faith in our words and our resident power. If we are taking about faith in God, then God is active and not our words.

Now in the morning, as they passed by, they saw the fig tree dried up from the roots. 21 And Peter, remembering, said to Him, "Rabbi, look! The fig tree which You cursed has withered away." 22 So Jesus answered and said to them, "Have faith in God. 23 For assuredly, I say to you, whoever says to this mountain, 'Be removed and be cast into the sea,' and does not doubt in his heart, but believes that those things he says will be done, he will have whatever he says. 24 Therefore I say to you, whatever things you ask when you pray, believe that you receive them, and you will have them. 25 And whenever you stand praying, if you have anything against anyone, forgive him, that your Father in heaven may also forgive you your trespasses. 26 But if you do not forgive, neither will your Father in heaven forgive your trespasses."

Mark 11:20-26

•SH: Good word, Berta. Romans 4:17 has been used to generate a whole new doctrine.

•RB: Big difference in faith in our faith and faith in God... We are all learning in this journey and these scriptures are really helpful. Thanks Berta

Pulling Scripture out of context lends to bad doctrine. Bad doctrine at best stunts growth, at worst promotes the work of Satan. Satan is the master at taking Scripture out of context. We wouldn't want someone to take our words out of context. Why do we do it to God?

Jesus Christ had two distinct natures—unmixed. Jesus, though God in the flesh, never tapped into divinity as He lived on this earth. Why then, do Christians seek to tap into an elevated God-man like persona? Though Jesus was one with the Father, and we too are one spirit with Lord (1 Corinthians 6:17), He never lived as God, instead He emptied Himself (Philippians 2:5-8). He lived as a man: He died as God.

Following is an excerpt from the Chalcedonian Creed, adopted at the Council of Chalcedon in AD 451:
(https://en.wikipedia.org/wiki/Chalcedonian_Definition)

"One and the Same Christ, Son, Lord, Only-begotten; acknowledged in Two Natures unconfusedly, unchangeably, indivisibly, inseparably; the difference of the Natures being in no way removed because of the Union, but rather the properties of each Nature being preserved, and (both) concurring into One Person and One Hypostasis; not as though He were parted or divided into Two Persons, but One and the Self-same Son and Only-begotten God, Word, Lord, Jesus Christ."

Matthew's Perspective

Following are examples from Matthew. I merely want to point out

Matthew's emphasis using a large enough sample of scriptures without rewriting the Gospel. As an introduction consider Jesus called:

- The Pharisees hypocrites (Matthew 16:3),
- Canaanite woman a dog (Matthew 15:26-28),
- The disciples little faiths (Matthew 16:8),
- His people a faithless and perverse generation (Matthew 17:17),
- The Scribes and Pharisees hypocrites, blinds leaders, and snakes (Matthew 23). Wow!

Did these scathing words spoken by Jesus bind the people who heard to a spiritual force set in motion by His words or was He merely declaring the obvious? In answer to these questions, let's further explore Matthew:

"It is enough for a disciple that he be like his teacher, and a servant like his master. If they have called the master of the house Beelzebub, how much more will they call those of his household! 26 Therefore do not fear them. For there is nothing covered that will not be revealed, and hidden that will not be known. 27 Whatever I tell you in the dark, speak in the light; and what you hear in the ear, preach on the housetops. 28 And do not fear those who kill the body but cannot kill the soul. But rather fear Him who is able to destroy both soul and body in hell."

Matthew 10:25-28

Jesus said they would call us Beelzebub, but we are not to fear them. He didn't say rebuke them, cleanse yourself from their curses, or break their words off. God obviously doesn't put much stock in the power of man to kill the soul. (Kill means "to kill in any way whatsoever.") Isn't the soul where words are supposed to take their murderous residency? Jesus says man doesn't have the power to kill the soul (Matthew 10:28). Instead of breaking their words off or rebuking them, Jesus said:

"But I say to you, love your enemies, bless those who curse you, do good to those who hate you, and pray for those who spitefully use you and persecute you, 45 that you may be sons of your Father in heaven; for He makes His sun rise on the evil and on the good, and sends rain on the just and on the unjust."

Matthew 5:44-45

Blessing those who curse us is the biblical counteraction to cursing. In the Parable of the Sower Jesus doesn't say anything about a curse or a negative word keeping the bad-soil heart from following God. He lays the responsibility on each individual person. Each one's own heart was the deciding factor as to whether or not they bore fruit to God and how much fruit they bore.

> "Therefore hear the parable of the sower: 19 When anyone hears the word of the kingdom, and does not understand it, then the wicked one comes and snatches away what was sown in his heart. This is he who received seed by the wayside. 20 But he who received the seed on stony places, this is he who hears the word and immediately receives it with joy; 21 yet he has no root in himself, but endures only for a while. For when tribulation or persecution arises because of the word, immediately he stumbles. 22 Now he who received seed among the thorns is he who hears the word, and the cares of this world and the deceitfulness of riches choke the word, and he becomes unfruitful. 23 But he who received seed on the good ground is he who hears the word and understands it, who indeed bears fruit and produces: some a hundredfold, some sixty, some thirty."
>
> Matthew 13:18-23

The reasons Jesus gives in the Parable of the Sower for not serving God:

1. Lacking understanding, so the devil steals it what was sown in their heart;
2. A hard heart, which easily stumbles at persecution and trial;
3. Cares of the world and love of wealth crowd out the word and this person becomes unfruitful.

The only soil bringing forth good fruit is:

4. Good soil within the heart, which brings forth varying degrees of fruit.

Did Jesus place a curse on the Pharisees by calling them blind leaders of the blind? Did His words bind them to this state of spiritual blindness or was it their unbelief and pride from within their own hearts? Remember Jesus said His words are spirit and life—all His words—even to the Pharisees. Jesus spoke truth. It was their choice whether or not to believe Him. They chose foolishly.

> When He had called the multitude to Himself, He said to them, "Hear and understand: 11 Not what goes into the mouth defiles a man; but what comes out of the mouth, this defiles a man." 12 Then His disciples came and said to Him, "Do You know that the Pharisees were offended when they heard this saying?" 13 But He answered and said, "Every plant which My heavenly Father has not planted will be

uprooted. 14 Let them alone. They are blind leaders of the blind. And if the blind leads the blind, both will fall into a ditch."

Matthew 15:10-14

"Do you not yet understand that whatever enters the mouth goes into the stomach and is eliminated? 18 But those things which proceed out of the mouth come from the heart, and they defile a man. 19 For out of the heart proceed evil thoughts, murders, adulteries, fornications, thefts, false witness, blasphemies. 20 These are the things which defile a man, but to eat with unwashed hands does not defile a man."

Matthew 15:17-20

Jesus said the heart of a man is what defiles the man. No mention of other's words defiling a man; apparently the human heart is wicked enough on its own.

Jesus didn't say people must first get words broken off of them, so that they are free enough, then they can follow Jesus. No, He said, "Deny yourself and follow Me."

Then Jesus said to His disciples, "If anyone desires to come after Me, let him deny himself, and take up his cross, and follow Me."

Matthew 16:24

"Desires" means "has a will to." If, therefore, anyone has a will to come after Jesus they must deny themselves. This means it is within each individual to follow Jesus. Free will is powerful and a God-given right inherent to each person. Even demons cannot over-ride an individual's will to come to Jesus. Self, however, can.

Though we have already looked at this story through Mark's eyes, it is advantageous to review it again from Matthew's:

Now in the morning, as He returned to the city, He was hungry. 19 And seeing a fig tree by the road, He came to it and found nothing on it but leaves, and said to it, "Let no fruit grow on you ever again." Immediately the fig tree withered away. 20 And when the disciples saw it, they marveled, saying, "How did the fig tree wither away so soon?" 21 So Jesus answered and said to them, "Assuredly, I say to you, if you have faith and do not doubt, you will not only do what was done to the fig tree, but also if you say to this mountain, 'Be removed and be cast into the sea,' it will be done. 22 And whatever things you ask in prayer, believing, you will receive."

Matthew 21:18-22

Here are the key points:

1. The subject is prayer and having faith [in God] that He will answer our prayers.
2. The fig tree was not a person.
3. Jesus only did and said what the Father instructed Him to do and say.
4. Our prayers, as Jesus' were, are to be according to the Father's will.

What we ask according to His will, we will have and not anything or everything we want. *Now this is the confidence that we have in Him, that if we ask anything according to His will, He hears us. 15 And if we know that He hears us, whatever we ask, we know that we have the petitions that we have asked of Him (1 John 5:14-15).* Note that God is the filter: we ask; He hears; He grants. And Philippians 4:6 says: *Be anxious for nothing, but in everything by prayer and supplication, with thanksgiving, let your requests be made known to God.* God is not just concerned about His will, but ours also. We may or may not get a "yes" from Him regarding our requests, but then do we really want everything we want? I think not. When we don't know His will, let's request to let Him know ours.

Peter, in Matthew 26, didn't just say: *"I do not know the Man,"* he also called curses upon himself and swore that he didn't know Jesus:

And a little later those who stood by came up and said to Peter, "Surely you also are one of them, for your speech betrays you." 74 Then he began to curse <2617> and swear, saying, "I do not know the Man!" Immediately a rooster crowed. 75 And Peter remembered the word of Jesus who had said to him, Before the rooster crows, you will deny Me three times." So he went out and wept bitterly.

Matthew 26:73-75

The Greek for "swear" means: "to swear with an oath and in swearing to call a person or thing as witness, to invoke, swear by." Therefore, Peter's words in verse 74 would be something comparable to, "Then he began to call dishonor, disgrace, and shame upon himself as he swore, with God as his witness, "I do not know the man, Jesus!" Yet, in reading the rest of the story we don't find any examples where Peter had curses broken off himself or that pronouncing curses on himself impacted him in any way. God didn't require a revocation, renouncement, or a sacrifice. Quite the opposite in fact! Peter was the one after the Resurrection who, when he saw the Lord on the beach, tore off his clothes and swam to Him.

I've heard many bizarre teachings concerning this story of Peter. A large family of churches' Bible teacher believed and taught that Peter received three curses when he denied Jesus three times. As a result, Peter tried to commit suicide when he saw Jesus on the shore. Instead of swimming to Jesus, Peter was actually swimming away from Jesus, attempting suicide. These curses were broken off Peter as he confessed he loved Jesus three times. Bizarre exegesis, right? Can sure feel the wind in that one!

Snap Shot from Mark

Jesus' explanation of the withered fig tree begins with, "have faith in God." He doesn't attribute man's words with the tree's demise:

> *As they were passing by in the morning, they saw the fig tree withered from the roots up. 21 Being reminded, Peter said to Him, "Rabbi, look, the fig tree which You cursed <2672> has withered." 22 And Jesus answered saying to them, "Have faith in God. 23 Truly I say to you, whoever says to this mountain, 'Be taken up and cast into the sea,' and does not doubt in his heart, but believes that what he says is going to happen, it will be granted him.'"*
>
> *Mark 11:20-23 (NASB)*

Note:
1. Have faith in God precedes: *"he will have whatever he says."* The object is not that we will have what we say, but rather that we are to have faith in God.
2. Jesus, our example, only said what He heard from the Father and did what He saw the Father doing.
3. *"... it will be granted him"* meaning, someone is granting. That someone is God. Therefore, God is directly involved, which also points back to: *"Have faith in God."*

We can't say things and then expect God will empower what we are saying. That is bad theology. If we could, wouldn't there be a significant amount of confusing supernatural things happening everywhere? I hear the decrees of Christians commanding things regularly that don't come to pass. Apparently their words don't carry power and apparently God isn't in the business of empowering their words: His words are spirit and life.

A Walk Though John

Jesus' words are spirit and life. God is the creator of all things through His spoken word; His words are spirit and life, not ours. [Jesus said:] *"It is the Spirit who gives life; the flesh profits nothing. The words that I speak to you are spirit, and they are life" (John 6:63).* Not our words, unless we are agreeing with what He is already saying. And even then, in truth, it's really His words. His words are spirit and life. *For by Him* ALL (emphasis mine) *things were created that are in heaven and that are on earth, visible and invisible, whether thrones or dominions or principalities or powers. All things were created through Him and for Him (Colossians 1: 16).* If all things are created by Him and for Him, how much room is left for mere men to create things with their words? Recall this next time you hear: *"Death and life are in the power of the tongue..." (Proverbs 18:21)* when someone proposes that mere man can create life and death through his words. I further discuss Proverbs 18:21 in this chapter's summary.

The next few scriptures from John reveal that Jesus and the Holy Spirit defer to the Father in what they say and what they do; they hear and see first what the Father is saying and doing, then do likewise. They are our ultimate examples. John 5:19 and John 5:30 are bedrock scriptures: they are foundational to everything we read in the NT. In them Jesus uses the words "nothing" and "whatever"; words that are all inclusive. They, therefore, silently watermark every page of the NT.[1]

From John:

> *Then Jesus answered and said to them, "Most assuredly, I say to you, the Son can do*

---

[1] See the subtitle "Watermarks" on page 94 for more on watermarks.

nothing of Himself, but what He sees the Father do; for whatever He does, the Son also does in like manner."

John 5:19

"I can of Myself do nothing. As I hear, I judge; and My judgment is righteous, because I do not seek My own will but the will of the Father who sent Me."

John 5:30

"For I have not spoken on My own authority; but the Father who sent Me gave Me a command, what I should say and what I should speak. 50 And I know that His command is everlasting life. Therefore, whatever I speak, just as the Father has told Me, so I speak."

John 12:49-50

"Do you not believe that I am in the Father, and the Father in Me? The words that I speak to you I do not speak on My own authority; but the Father who dwells in Me does the works. 11 Believe Me that I am in the Father and the Father in Me, or else believe Me for the sake of the works themselves."

"12 Most assuredly, I say to you, he who believes in Me, the works that I do he will do also; and greater works than these he will do, because I go to My Father. 13 And whatever you ask in My name, that I will do, that the Father may be glorified in the Son. 14 If you ask anything in My name, I will do it."

John 14:10-14

"However, when He, the Spirit of truth, has come, He will guide you into all truth; for He will not speak on His own authority, but whatever He hears He will speak; and He will tell you things to come. 14 He will glorify Me, for He will take of what is Mine and declare it to you. 15 All things that the Father has are Mine. Therefore I said that He will take of Mine and declare it to you."

John 16:13-15

Again, both the Holy Spirit and Jesus only followed the Father's leading. Yet, the Bible doesn't always make statements like "Jesus heard the Father say, "_____" so He said, "_____." Or "Jesus saw the Father healing the blind man so Jesus healed him." The Bible makes statements like John 5:19 and John 5:30 and then expects us to view all other scriptures within their parameters. Viewing scriptures outside these parameters lends to, not only to confusion surrounding the power of mankind's words, but misunderstanding about many things. We must take scriptures like these from John and build our doctrines upon them:

laying the foundation first, then building from that foundation. God requires that we engage with Him in prayer, and He in turn impresses upon us what to pray. Therefore, as we pray we are praying according to His will. Subsequently when we pray, hearing first, we receive what we have asked. When we pray—hearing first—we are praying according to His will. Furthermore, as we engage with Him, He purifies our hearts to be like His. Thus, His desires become our desires. This is how scriptures like James 4:2-3 and Mark 11:24 are reconciled. Granted, He also says in Philippians: *Be anxious for nothing, but in everything by prayer and supplication, with thanksgiving, let your requests be made known to God (Philippians 4:6)*. He loves the conversation.

Acts and the Epistles

When the epistles talk about people's words, particularly Christians' words, they are usually in the context of whether or not the words are springing from a carnal mindset or a spiritual mindset; if they are edifying and truthful; if they are prompted by the Holy Spirit or not. Many times we see warnings about words—as the speaker and not the hearer. (Both Mark 4:24 and Luke 8:18 are in the context of hearing God.) James 5:9, for example, shows that the Judge will judge the one who complains against another: *Do not grumble against one another, brethren, lest you be condemned. Behold, the Judge is standing at the door!* Notice how the emphasis is again on the speaker? James 5:9 sounds just like Jesus' words in Matthew 12: *"But I say to you that for every idle word men may speak, they will give account of it in the day of judgment. 37 For by your words you will be justified, and by your words you will be condemned" (Matthew 12:36-37)*. The speaker suffers the consequences from the Judge. Yes, we are to correct one another in love and speak the truth in love, but the Bible does not instruct us to come against words themselves. Only if we eat and digest words will they have power to influence us.

Many stories are contained within the pages of Acts. The church had begun. The Gospel was preached and the Holy Spirit was moving dynamically through His people with signs and wonders. Acts opens its curtains in 1:1-2 with:

The former account I made, O Theophilus, of all that Jesus began both to do and teach, 2 until the day in which He was taken up, after He through the Holy Spirit had given commandments to the apostles whom He had chosen.

Acts 1:1-2

Acts' opening statement paints a beautiful portrait for what is to be written therein about the early church: we see Jesus yielding to the Holy Spirit's leading as He, through the Holy Spirit, gave the commandments to the apostles. The Holy Spirit came upon Jesus at the beginning of His ministry and He yielded to Him throughout its entirety. Acts 1:8 identifies the power the church would receive as the Holy Spirit came upon them. Then, at the beginning of the church age, He sent into His church the fulfillment of Pentecost that they too could live as He had lived—yielded to and empowered by the Holy Spirit. Acts 2 dynamically displays the fulfillment of Pentecost with the Holy Spirit's powerful coming.

In Acts 8 we read the story of Simon the sorcerer. The chain of events are as follows:

1. Phillip goes to Samaria.
2. He preaches Christ and performs miracles.
3. Many believe and receive Jesus.
4. Many are delivered from demons and healed.
5. Many are baptized.
6. Simon (the sorcerer) believed and was baptized.
7. Simon is amazed as Phillip does signs and miracles.
8. Jerusalem apostles hear and send John and Peter.
9. Peter and John lay hands on the Samarian believers to minister the Baptism of the Holy Spirit to them.
10. Simon (the sorcerer) tries to buy the power to lay hands on people that they would receive the Holy Spirit.

Acts 8 continues:

But Peter said to him, "Your money perish with you, because you thought that the gift of God could be purchased with money! 21 You have neither part nor portion in this matter, for your heart is not right in the sight of God. 22 Repent therefore of this your wickedness, and pray God if perhaps the thought of your heart may be forgiven you. 23 For I see that you are poisoned by bitterness and bound by iniquity." 24 Then Simon answered and said, "Pray to the Lord for me, that none of the things which you have spoken may come upon me."

Acts 8:20-24

We just read about a sorcerer who received Jesus. Simon was such a powerful sorcerer that the whole city followed him. Then he was born again and baptized. Yet, Peter breaks nothing off Simon—no words, no powers, no curses—nothing—even after Peter said: *"Your money perish with you…"* to Simon. Rather, Simon is told (remember Simon received Jesus Christ and was baptized in verse 13) to repent and pray to the Lord. Peter apparently saw into Simon's heart by a word of knowledge and pinpointed Simon's deep rooted bitterness and bondage. But even then Peter didn't break bitterness and bondage off Simon. Peter instead tells him to repent and pray. To the newly saved former sorcerer Peter says: "repent and pray"! Then Simon asks for prayer. Prayer and repentance, for this believer, was the answer to sin and bondage, bondage likely from demonic influences from Simon's past!

Acts 13 gives an account of Paul's interaction with a Jewish false prophet, Elymas, and Sergius Paulus, the proconsul. Elymas tried to keep the proconsul from faith in Jesus Christ, but his magic and words did not contain the power to do so. In the end the proconsul became a believer.

Now when they had gone through the island to Paphos, they found a certain sorcerer, a false prophet, a Jew whose name was Bar-Jesus, 7 who was with the proconsul, Sergius Paulus, an intelligent man. This man called for Barnabas and Saul and sought to hear the word of God. 8 But Elymas the sorcerer (for so his name is translated) withstood them, seeking to turn the proconsul away from the faith. 9 Then Saul, who also is called Paul, filled with the Holy Spirit, looked intently at him 10 and said, "O full of all deceit and all fraud, you son of the devil, you enemy of all righteousness, will you not cease perverting the straight ways of the Lord? 11 And now, indeed, the hand of the Lord is upon you, and you shall be blind, not seeing the sun for a time." And immediately a dark mist fell on him, and he went around seeking someone to lead him by the hand. 12 Then the proconsul believed, when he saw what had been done, being astonished at the teaching of the Lord.

Acts 13:6-12

Paul, motivated by the Holy Spirit, called Elymas: *"full of all deceit and fraud, a son of the devil, an enemy of all righteousness…And now, indeed, the hand of the Lord is upon you, and you shall be blind, not seeing the sun for a time."* Immediately Elymas was blind. Remember that when Paul met Jesus for the first time he too was struck blind. Paul knew the impact blindness had on him—it took blindness for him to truly see. Though this is conjecture, I bet this was the Lord's intent with Elymas. It wasn't Paul's power that blinded Elymas, for it was the hand of the Lord, as stated by Paul (verse 11).

Moving on from Acts to the epistles, we will begin with Paul's first letter to the Corinthians:

> *And my speech and my preaching were not with persuasive words of human wisdom, but in demonstration of the Spirit and of power, 5 that your faith should not be in the wisdom of men but in the power of God.*
>
> *1 Corinthians 2:4-5*

If words or declarations carried inherent power, these statements would be unnecessary. Words and power would be equal. And yet, the Holy Spirit is necessary for the message to be preached as God intended:

> *But I [Paul] will come to you shortly, if the Lord wills, and I will know, not the word of those who are puffed up, but the power. 20 For the kingdom of God is not in word but in power.*
>
> *1 Corinthians 4:19*

Paul, by the Holy Spirit, made a definitive statement concerning words: people's words alone do not have power. Even preaching the Gospel, *which is the power of God to salvation for everyone who believes (Romans 1:16),* is to be with power and not words only.

In Ephesians the wording is directed to the speaker:

> *Let no corrupt word proceed out of your mouth, but what is good for necessary edification, that it may impart grace to the hearers. 30 And do not grieve the Holy Spirit of God, by whom you were sealed for the day of redemption. 31 Let all*

bitterness, wrath, anger, clamor, and evil speaking be put away from you, with all malice. 32 And be kind to one another, tenderhearted, forgiving one another, just as God in Christ forgave you.

Ephesians 4:29-32

Straightforward, right? God doesn't say that if we talk like this we are impregnating the atmosphere with hurtful words that will bind people, as some people teach. No, God is saying Christians should talk appropriately. Our intent should be to edify and minister grace. (Impart in the Greek does not render a supernatural impartation.) Who would want to grieve the Holy Spirit? Out of our heart flow our words. Get the heart right and the words will follow.

Paul's instruction to Timothy concerning rescuing a devil's captive is a truth encounter: a correction leading to knowledge leading to freedom:

And a servant of the Lord must not quarrel but be gentle to all, able to teach, patient, 25 in humility correcting those who are in opposition, if God perhaps will grant them repentance, so that they may know the truth, 26 and that they may come to their senses and escape the snare of the devil, having been taken captive by him to do his will.

2 Timothy 2:24-26

Breaking curses, breaking demonic ties, or soul ties (which aren't biblical) aren't even hinted at here either. Truth—it's an encounter with the truth. God's truth is enough. Recall, Jesus said His words were spirit and life. Accompanying God's word is God's Spirit. God's word that is in context and rightly handled. We can, but it isn't best, to just throw out a scripture or two. It is best to hear God in the moment and be led by His Spirit when leading captives out of their devil prison.

The NT does not give people the power to wield the hearts of others beyond soul to soul influence. I talk a great deal more about this in the next chapter, Chapter 2—Mortals' Curses. Lest we forget, even demons could not keep their captive from running to Jesus. The man with Legion ran to Jesus, bowed down before Him, and was delivered (Luke 5:6). People influence others by their words. But people only have control over others by their words if the recipient yields to, believes in, and then takes to heart the words spoken to them and makes the words their own.

Summary

O LORD, I know the way of man is not in himself; It is not in man who walks to direct his own steps (Jeremiah 10:23). If man doesn't even own his own steps, how in the realm of possibilities could his words possibly carry the power to dictate the steps of others'?

Chapter 2

Considerations

Concerning Authority

W HAT WAS IT ABOUT THE CENTURION'S faith that made Jesus marvel? The centurion's conclusion:

> *"Therefore I did not even think myself worthy to come to You. But say the word, and my servant will be healed. 8 For I also am a man placed under authority, having soldiers under me. And I say to one, 'Go,' and he goes; and to another, 'Come,' and he comes; and to my servant, 'Do this,' and he does it." 9 When Jesus heard these things, He marveled at him, and turned around and said to the crowd that followed Him, "I say to you, I have not found such great faith, not even in Israel!"*
>
> *Luke 7:7b-9*

Jesus recognized the centurion's understanding of authority was the same as Jesus' authority with the Father. He understood his ability to give commands to those under him and have those orders carried out. He knew all it took was a word. Not because the word had power, but, rather, because of the one giving the command to be carried out had the authority to do so. The one under him was not functioning on his own authority; he was only carrying out the order of another. Jesus marveled when He saw that the centurion understood authority, for this is how the Kingdom of God operates. Faith is directly related to understanding authority. Jesus said in John 14:10: *"Do you not believe that I am in the Father, and the Father in Me? The words that I speak to you I do not speak on My own authority; but the Father who dwells in Me does the works."* Though the Father was in Jesus, as the Holy Spirit is in us, Jesus still said it was the Father doing the work. This is unequivocally the same way the centurion understood authority, faith, and words.

Jesus discusses this again in John 12: *"For I have not spoken on My own authority; but the Father who sent Me gave Me a command, what I should say and what I should speak. 50 And I know that His command is everlasting life. Therefore, whatever I speak, just as the Father has told Me, so I speak"* (John 12:49-50). When Jesus spoke or acted, He wasn't initiating, rather He was obeying the Father. Carrying out the will of Another. This is the paradigm of the Kingdom. It is the correct way to view the power of words. Our words have power when they are first Someone else's words—His.

Mark 16 is post resurrection. If Mark 16 ended with verse 18 there would be room for ambiguity, but Mark continues:

> *"And these signs will follow those who believe: In My name they will cast out demons; they will speak with new tongues; 18 they will take up serpents; and if they drink anything deadly, it will by no means hurt them; they will lay hands on the sick, and they will recover.*
> *19 So then, after the Lord had spoken to them, He was received up into heaven, and sat down at the right hand of God. 20 And they went out and preached everywhere, the Lord working with them and confirming the word through the accompanying signs. Amen."*
>
> Mark 16:17-20

Verse 20 reveals that the Lord worked with them and was the one confirming the word with the signs that followed. Again, we speak and God does the works. Why use the name of Jesus if all we have to do is speak? His name is tied to His Person. His Person is present in His name. The end of Mark states: *"...these signs will follow those who believe: In My name they will..."* It is "in His name..." Some believe we have resident power to wield Jesus' name kind of like magic, though they would never admit it. Granted, when scriptures are taken out of context, they can seem to bend towards this wielding of power. But context matters. Let's not manipulate the word to fit our theology, instead let it form ours. Additionally, some avow that the earth and its elements are subject to us for no other reason than because the Holy Spirit lives in us. This doctrine claims we have authority over creation as a new creation in Christ. A regained authority, once lost in the Garden, and not God presently active working through us—an inherent deposit, if you will. This deposit, they believe, restores the authority Adam forfeited when he fell, taking all mankind with him. (For more on this, see Concerning Ruling over Creation on page 50.) Following are a few examples of when the earth was spoken to and it obeyed:

- Elijah stopped the rain for three years. Albeit Elijah did everything at God's command (1 Kings 18:36).
- Jesus stilled the storm; He too did everything just as He saw the Father do (John 5:19).
- The Lord turned the sun's shadow back for Hezekiah (Isaiah 38).
- The sun stood still at the command of Joshua. Or was it God? Carefully reading Joshua 10, it is God the Lord who listened to the voice of a man and fought for Israel. Yes, Joshua spoke, nevertheless his words did not stop the sun, God did.

The truth is God uses people. Some believe He does nothing without using people. That is ridiculous! Where were people when He created in Genesis 1? It is true, nevertheless, He uses us. In fact, unless we lay hands on the sick, they may not recover. Unless we pray, God may not move. Unless we hear the Holy Spirit then speak, God may not act. He uses people. He uses us. This is the truth.

Concerning Proverbs 18:21

Now let's tackle Proverbs 18:21: *Death and life are in the power of the tongue, And those who love it will eat its fruit.*

I cannot remember a time when I heard this scripture quoted in its entirety, and therefore presented accurately. To surmise that people have power to command life and death with their words is not what this scripture is saying. First of all it is a proverb. We cannot form a doctrine on a proverb. Furthermore, the focus of Proverbs 18:21 is on "those who love the power of the tongue." It is pointing to the speaker—the speaker is the reaper of the words. *"Those who love it"* is the speaker; *"will eat its fruit,"* meaning those who love to wag their tongue will reap the consequences of their own words. The New Living Translation (NLT) provides clarity: *The tongue can bring death or life; those who love to talk will reap the consequences.* I looked at eight commentaries and all agree with the NLT's translation. Also, Proverbs 18:21 aligns perfectly with Matthew 12:34-37. In Matthew, Jesus said it was the speaker who would receive the ramifications of what they say.

> *"Brood of vipers! How can you, being evil, speak good things? For out of the abundance of the heart the mouth speaks. 35 A good man out of the good treasure of his heart brings forth good things, and an evil man out of the evil treasure brings forth evil things. 36 But I say to you that for every idle word men may speak, they will give account of it in the day of judgment. 37 For by your words you will be justified, and by your words you will be condemned."*
>
> Matthew 12:34-37

In the Garden, Satan told Eve she could be like God if she ate the fruit. Could it be that some Christians fall for the same lie Eve believed in the Garden? God's words are creative. He can create something out of nothing just by speaking. Can a man do that? Can the devil? Or is this a uniqueness belonging only to God? Some purport procreation proves mankind has creative ability within himself. Is procreation creating? God said the seed was within itself (Genesis 1:11-12). So do plants have creative power? Do cows or horses or cats or dogs have creative power? This, then, would be the logical conclusion, would it not?

Concerning Confession Leading to Salvation

Many people believe confession is what solidifies salvation. The seal, if you will. That without confession (words actually coming out your mouth) there is no salvation. Romans 10:9 stands stately promoting this stance: *...that if you confess with your mouth the Lord Jesus and believe in your heart that God has raised Him from the dead, you will be saved.* Romans 10:9 is only one of many scriptures showing how someone receives salvation. Following are scriptures where confession is not noted:

- *"For God so loved the world that He gave His only begotten Son, that whoever believes in Him should not perish but have everlasting life" (John 3:16).*

- *Then he said to Jesus, "Lord, remember me when You come into Your kingdom." 43 And Jesus said to him, "Assuredly, I say to you, today you will be with Me in Paradise" (Luke 23:42-43).* Though this man spoke about Jesus' innocence and His Kingdom, he never confessed "Jesus as Lord."
- *But as many as received Him, to them He gave the right to become children of God, to those who believe in His name... (John 1:12).*
- *Now a certain woman named Lydia heard us. She was a seller of purple from the city of Thyatira, who worshiped God. The Lord opened her heart to heed the things spoken by Paul (Acts 16:14).* Though not directly saying Lydia received Jesus, we know the Lord opened her heart to respond to the things spoken by Paul. She and her household were then baptized, which normally follows salvation.
- *So they [Paul and Silas] said, "Believe on the Lord Jesus Christ, and you will be saved, you and your household" (Acts 16:31).*
- *But even to this day, when Moses is read, a veil lies on their heart. 16 Nevertheless when one turns to the Lord, the veil is taken away (2 Corinthians 3:15-16).*

Concerning Ruling over Creation

Do Christians have authority over creation, i.e. storms, weather, mountains, and fig trees? Pursuing answers to these questions necessitates understanding God's original job description for Adam, in the Garden, as a man created in the image of God. Who was Adam originally? Additionally, how do we view Adam and his job description through the lens of the Fall, the New Covenant, and throughout the Millennial age? This section answers these vital questions; vital, for they become foundational to understanding the next two sections on the created beings of humanity and of witchcraft.

Let's explore the original Adam: the Adam in the Garden, made in the image of God. After God had finished Creation, Genesis 1:31 states: *Then God saw everything that He had made, and indeed it was very good. So the evening and the morning were the sixth day.* God had told Adam in 1:28 to: *"Be fruitful and multiply; fill the earth and subdue it; have dominion over the fish of the sea, over the birds of the air, and over every living thing that moves on the earth."* However, Post-Fall Genesis says:

"...Cursed <0779> is the ground for your sake; In toil you shall eat of it All the days of your life. 18 Both thorns and thistles it shall bring forth for you, And you shall eat the herb of the field. 19 In the sweat of your face you shall eat bread Till you return to the ground, For out of it you were taken; For dust you are, And to dust you shall return."
Genesis 3:17b-19

A vast change occurred. Creation fell; death entered; chaos ensued. The earth, what it produced, and the animal kingdom fell with Adam. Adam, previous to the fall had been told to subdue the earth and rule. But they were now banished from the Garden where Adam was told to rule. Was it even now possible? Banned from the Garden, their new land would grow thorns and thistles. Animals would prey; animals were prey. Everything fell; everything changed. God had told Adam to rule pre-Fall, while still in the Garden. But now he was exiled and thorns and thistles would populate his home.

Points to note:

- *"Be fruitful and multiply; fill the earth and subdue it"* was spoken about:
    - fish of the sea, and
    - over the birds of the sky, and
    - over every living thing moving on the earth.
- *"Be fruitful and multiply; fill the earth (land)"* is related to *"subdue it."* Not to Adam alone, but also included those who would be born to Adam and after him.
- Humanity would rule in harmony with creation in a state of perfection.
- Sin was absent.
- Chaos was absent.
- Death was absent.

Thus, the ethos wherein Adam and Eve were told to rule was sin-free and death-free. We likely all agree Adam and Eve lost their right to rule in the fall. Not taken away by God, but rather, handed over to Satan through intrigue. Was it regained through the Cross? During this current age, His kingdom is manifested as we work with the Holy Spirit to display the characteristics of His kingdom to come. We rule and reign with Him in this age in part, howbeit in fullness in the next age. Jesus will sit on His

Throne in New Jerusalem during the Millennial Age. The kingdom of God will be on Earth, and its King will rule.

We have authority over creation in this age as we hear God, then speak. Jesus patterned this. Moses patterned this, even while under the Old Covenant. Hearing, then speaking leading to authority may seem obvious, and yet some teach that ruling the earth would take superhuman ability. Therefore, they conclude, Adam must have had supernatural abilities that became dormant in the Fall. These superhuman abilities, they believe, again become inherent or alive or awakened in regeneration through the new birth. If true, such a perspective would make reliance on the Holy Spirit unnecessary, would it not?

Concerning the Created Being

What about "The Latent Power of the Soul" about which Watchman Nee writes? In the Garden, God created man. It was here that God said everything He created was very good. Mankind as He created them was very good. Mankind was in their original sinless state. And yet there was no evidence of what we would consider superhuman power. Now consider, the Second Adam, Jesus, the sinless One. He never tapped into a superhuman power—a latent power of the soul. In fact Jesus said three times in John that He did nothing of Himself (John 5:19, 5:30, and 8:28). Reason with me for a moment: if there is a latent power of the soul or spirit, then in a sinless state it would not be forbidden. God would have created it within mankind in the beginning and then stated it was very good. Jesus also would not have considered it to be forbidden for He would have been the One who endowed mankind with such power. We must, therefore, conclude it does not exist and that mankind is dependent upon either God or the devil for supernatural power.

Concerning Witchcraft/Sorcery/Magic

So what about witchcraft? Could witchcraft belong to a resident latent power within mankind? What does Galatians 5:20 mean when it states witchcraft is a work of the flesh? What about Pharaoh's magicians? We will look at 2 Thessalonians 2:8-10 and Revelation 13 for answers:

And then the lawless one will be revealed, whom the Lord will consume with the breath of His mouth and destroy with the brightness of His coming. 9 The coming of the lawless one is according to the working of Satan, with all power, signs, and lying wonders, 10 and with all unrighteous deception among those who perish, because they did not receive the love of the truth, that they might be saved.

2 Thessalonians 2:8-10

Consider the wording: *"The coming of the lawless one is according to the working of Satan, with all power, signs, and lying wonders, and with all unrighteous deception among those who perish..."*

Revelation 13 deals with 4 individuals: the dragon, the 1st beast, another beast (2nd beast), and God. Following are the key points of the chapter.

- The dragon is Satan (Revelation 12:9 and 20:2)
- Satan gave the 1st beast:
  - his power
  - his throne
  - great authority
- People worshiped Satan through the 1st beast
- 1st beast was given authority over people for 42 months
- 2nd beast exercises all the authority of the 1st beast and makes the earth worship the 1st beast
- 2nd beast performs great signs and makes fire come down out of heaven to the earth
- 2nd beast deceives those who dwell on the earth because of the signs which he performed
- It was given to the 2nd beast to give breath to the image of the beast, so that the image of the beast would speak
- The 2nd beast forced people to worship the 1st beast

The 1st beast and his counterpart, the 2nd beast, are the two most supernaturally evil people the earth will ever meet. Their inspiration and authority are bestowed by Satan. Through them Satan deceives the whole earth with lying signs and wonders, and through force. 2 Thessalonians specifically says that the work is: *according to the working of Satan, with all power, signs, and lying wonders, and with all unrighteous deception...* These two did not have power within themselves to perform lying signs and wonders, instead is was conferred upon them by Satan. To reiterate

Revelation 13, the dragon (Satan): *gave him* (the 1st beast) *his power and his throne and great authority*. Satan therefore must have it to give.

Throughout the Bible we see demonic activity associated with idol worship, including worship to the image of the beast in Revelation 13. We see lying signs and wonders also directly granted by Satan himself. The Egyptian magicians and sorcerers were worshippers of foreign gods and displayed lying signs and wonders. Galatians 5:20 states that witchcraft/sorcery is a work of the flesh. This does not mean that the flesh can produce magic, rather it means that magic/witchcraft/sorcery are tied to the will of the flesh and not to the Holy Spirit. Just as the flesh prompts someone towards outbursts of anger or adultery or drunkenness, it also prompts people to entertain powers from demonic sources. Witchcraft, magic, and sorcery are always tied to a demonic source. Man does not possess within himself the latent power of the soul.

Since people don't possess independent spiritual power, they must have another source, and there are only two: God or Satan. The Greek word for sorcery (pharmakeia) in Galatians 5:20 is tied to idolatry, drugs, and sorcery. It carries the definition, "sorcery, magical arts, often found in connection with idolatry and fostered by it." Idolatry is clearly tied to demons (1 Corinthians 10:20), as is fortune-telling (Acts 16:16-18). The slave-girl in Acts 16 had a spirit of divination driven out of her.

Consider, occult practices like charms, tarot cards, idolatry, potions, spells, mysticism, Spiritism, false religions, and the like are portals into the demonic realm. They entice and attract demons. Sorcery is always in connection with idolatry. It must be so. For all worship and religions apart from the one true YHWH are forms of idolatry. This is true whether humanism, Satanism, cults, deism, or atheism—any religion (loosely used) apart from the one true God is idolatry. Therefore, they are all under the power and influence of demons and Satan. Satan, the deceiver, will and does use anything to grip the heart of man away from the living God. This is idolatry. Idolatry is always watermarked with Satan. He is always behind the curtain. As 1 John 5:19 states: *We know that we are of God, and that the whole world lies in the power of the evil one.*

Chapter 3

Mortals' Curses

Words Spoken To or Against God's People

IN THE LAST CHAPTER WE LOOKED at the speaker's words and the power they carry. This chapter presents clear exegesis regarding curses and the power of words spoken to or over another, specifically regarding God's people. We will consider both those under the Old Covenant and the New Covenant. Can words have supernatural power over us? This chapter, Mortals' Curses, presents God's perspective on words spoken both to and against His people. Looking forward, Chapter 4 divulges who the author of curses is and why.

Old Testament

Abraham

As people dealt with Abraham, God would deal with them:

> Now the LORD said to Abram, "Go forth from your country, And from your relatives And from your father's house, To the land which I will show you; 2 And I will make you a great nation, And I will bless you, And make your name great; And so you shall be a blessing; 3 And I will bless those who bless you, And the one who curses <07043> you I will curse <0779>. And in you all the families of the earth will be blessed."
>
> *Genesis 12:1-3*

Abraham wasn't told to have curses broken off of himself. God said He would curse those who cursed Abraham. Paraphrasing, "I'll take care of it Abraham, you just focus on Me. I'll repay everyone for how they treat you and for what they say to you."

Saul and Jonathan

Saul as the king had the right and authority to make the edict that he did. Saul decreed that anyone who ate food would be cursed. However, as the story of Jonathan continued Saul tried to enforce his decree by killing Jonathan. The people stopped him. The pronounced curse, even from the king, did not have the power to rule over Jonathan:

> Now the men of Israel were hard-pressed on that day, for Saul had put the people under oath, saying, "Cursed <0779> be the man who eats food before evening, and until I have avenged myself on my enemies." So none of the people tasted food. 25 All the people of the land entered the forest, and there was honey on the ground. 26 When the people entered the forest, behold, there was a flow of honey; but no man put his hand to his mouth, for the people feared the oath. 27 But Jonathan had not heard when his father put the people under oath; therefore, he put out the end of the staff that was in his hand and dipped it in the honeycomb, and put his hand to his mouth, and his eyes brightened. 28 Then one of the people said, "Your father strictly put the people under oath, saying, 'Cursed <0779> be the man who eats food today.'" And the people were weary. 29 Then Jonathan said, "My father has troubled the land. See now, how my eyes have brightened because I tasted a little of this honey. 30 How much more, if only the people had eaten freely today of the spoil of their enemies which they found! For now the slaughter among the Philistines has not been great."
>
> 1 Samuel 14:24-30

David cursed by Shimei

David didn't try to stop Shimei, rebuke a devil, or try to kill Shimei. It appears David was disinterested in the cursing and more interested in the dealings of God in his life, for he said:

> "It may be that the LORD will look on my affliction, and that the LORD will repay me with good for his cursing <07045> this day" (:12).Now when King David came to Bahurim, there was a man from the family of the house of Saul, whose name was Shimei the son of Gera, coming from there. He came out, cursing <07043>

continuously as he came. 6 And he threw stones at David and at all the servants of King David. And all the people and all the mighty men were on his right hand and on his left. 7 Also Shimei said thus when he cursed <07043>: "Come out! Come out! You bloodthirsty man, you rogue! 8 The LORD has brought upon you all the blood of the house of Saul, in whose place you have reigned; and the LORD has delivered the kingdom into the hand of Absalom your son. So now you are caught in your own evil, because you are a bloodthirsty man!" 9 Then Abishai the son of Zeruiah said to the king, "Why should this dead dog curse <07043> my lord the king? Please, let me go over and take off his head!" 10 But the king said, "What have I to do with you, you sons of Zeruiah? So let him curse <07043>, because the LORD has said to him, 'Curse <07043> David.' Who then shall say, 'Why have you done so?' " 11 And David said to Abishai and all his servants, "See how my son who came from my own body seeks my life. How much more now may this Benjamite? Let him alone, and let him curse <07043> for so the LORD has ordered him. 12 It may be that the LORD will look on my affliction, and that the LORD will repay me with good for his cursing <07045> this day." 13 And as David and his men went along the road, Shimei went along the hillside opposite him and cursed <07043> as he went, threw stones at him and kicked up dust.

2 Samuel 16:5-13

Later Shimei repented to David and David swore he would not have him put to death. What was David's composure toward Shimei and his cursing? David committed himself to God. He knew God was sovereign and reasoned God had allowed Shimei to curse. David knew God could turn the attempted curse into a blessing. In fact, David knew that if there was power in the curse that it would have to had been initiated by God, and thus Shimei would only be repeating what the LORD had said (:10). However, Shimei's words had no influence on David. Absalom died and David became King of all Israel. In the end, God turned the curse of Shimei back upon himself. As David knew he was about to die, David said to Solomon: *"do not hold him [Shimei] guiltless"* (1 Kings 2:9):

"And see, you have with you Shimei the son of Gera, a Benjamite from Bahurim, who cursed me with a malicious curse in the day when I went to Mahanaim. But he came down to meet me at the Jordan, and I swore to him by the LORD, saying, 'I will not put you to death with the sword.' 9 Now therefore, do not hold him guiltless, for you are a wise man and know what you ought to do to him; but bring his gray hair down to the grave with blood."

1 Kings 2:8-9

The cursing Shimei spoke to David, God brought back upon Shimei. David's view of people's cursing him and his attitude toward them is again seen in Psalms 109:

> 17 As he [unknown individual] loved cursing <07045>, so let it come to him; As he did not delight in blessing, so let it be far from him. 18 As he clothed himself with cursing <07045> as with his garment, So let it enter his body like water, And like oil into his bones. 19 Let it be to him like the garment which covers him, And for a belt with which he girds himself continually... "Help me, O LORD my God; Save me according to Your lovingkindness. 27 And let them know that this is Your hand; You, LORD, have done it. 28 Let them curse <07043>, but You bless; When they arise, they shall be ashamed, But Your servant shall be glad. 29 Let my accusers be clothed with dishonor, And let them cover themselves with their own shame as with a robe.
>
> Psalm 109:17-20, 26-29

This was David's perspective about this one who: "clothed himself with cursing as with his garment (:18)." David knew that the LORD would repay those who cursed him and that this cursing would never touch him. He knew, instead, their cursing would enter their own being like water, penetrating like oil; they loved cursing so they received it. David wasn't concerned with what people said to him, because he committed himself to God. He knew God. He knew God would turn their cursing into a blessing for him. This was David's confidence and the confidence of the children of Israel throughout the OT. It should be ours.

Hezekiah and Sennacherib, King of Assyria

Nothing said to Hezekiah from the king of Assyria—his threats and accusations—bore fruit. In fact, God took it all very personally:

> And so it was, when King Hezekiah heard it, that he tore his clothes, covered himself with sackcloth, and went into the house of the LORD. 2 Then he sent Eliakim, who was over the household, Shebna the scribe, and the elders of the priests, covered with sackcloth, to Isaiah the prophet, the son of Amoz. 3 And they said to him, "Thus says Hezekiah: 'This day is a day of trouble, and rebuke, and blasphemy; for the children have come to birth, but there is no strength to bring them forth. 4 'It may be that the LORD your God will hear all the words of the Rabshakeh, whom his master the king of Assyria has sent to reproach the living God, and will rebuke the words which the LORD your God has heard. Therefore lift up your prayer for the remnant that is left.'"

5 So the servants of King Hezekiah came to Isaiah. 6 And Isaiah said to them, "Thus you shall say to your master, 'Thus says the LORD: "Do not be afraid of the words which you have heard, with which the servants of the king of Assyria have blasphemed Me. 7 Surely I will send a spirit upon him, and he shall hear a rumor and return to his own land; and I will cause him to fall by the sword in his own land."'"

2 Kings 19:1-7

Hezekiah took the words of the Assyrian king and laid them out before the Lord (2 Kings 19:14-19). The Lord delivered Judah and repaid Sennacherib. Sennacherib heard a rumor, returned to his own land, and was killed just as God had said through Isaiah the prophet.

Nehemiah, Tobiah, Sanballat ...and God

Sanballat the Horonite, Tobiah the Ammonite official, and Geshem the Arab, caused many problems for Nehemiah. Nevertheless, none of their words, plots against his life, tactics to stop his work, or other conspiracies worked against Nehemiah:

But it so happened, when Sanballat heard that we were rebuilding the wall, that he was furious and very indignant, and mocked the Jews. 2 And he spoke before his brethren and the army of Samaria, and said, "What are these feeble Jews doing? Will they fortify themselves? Will they offer sacrifices? Will they complete it in a day? Will they revive the stones from the heaps of rubbish — stones that are burned?" 3 Now Tobiah the Ammonite was beside him, and he said, "Whatever they build, if even a fox goes up on it, he will break down their stone wall."4 Hear, O our God, for we are despised; turn their reproach on their own heads, and give them as plunder to a land of captivity! 5 Do not cover their iniquity, and do not let their sin be blotted out from before You; for they have provoked You to anger before the builders. 6 So we built the wall, and the entire wall was joined together up to half its height, for the people had a mind to work.

Nehemiah 4:1-6

Even though their words demoralized the builders, in the end their enemies recognized the hand of God was with the Jews. The result was: *And it happened, when all our enemies heard of it [the completion of the wall], and all the nations around us saw these things, that they were very disheartened in their own eyes; for they perceived that this work was done by our God (Nehemiah 6:16).*

Balaam

Previously we looked at Balaam the prophet. Recall he wanted to curse the Israelites for money. A prophet for profit.

> *And God said to Balaam, "You shall not go with them; you shall not curse <0779> the people, for they are blessed."*
>
> *Numbers 22:12*

When someone is blessed by God, who or what can overpower Him? Remember we are under the New Covenant. We are a blessed people in Christ, children of the living God, a royal priesthood—we are blessed with every spiritual blessing in Christ.

God to New Covenant People

Isaiah must be speaking about New Covenant people for they are the only people in whose heart is God's law:

> *"Listen to Me, you who know righteousness, You people in whose heart is My law: Do not fear the reproach of men, Nor be afraid of their insults. 8 For the moth will eat them up like a garment, And the worm will eat them like wool; But My righteousness will be forever, And My salvation from generation to generation."*
>
> *Isaiah 51:7-8*

From God's point of view, men's words don't impact His people. God didn't even say to come against their words. He appears to endorse ignoring them. Why? Because He will repay and He has the power to do so.

Jeremiah

> *Woe is me, my mother, That you have borne me, A man of strife and a man of contention to the whole earth! I have neither lent for interest, Nor have men lent to me for interest. Every one of them curses <07043> me.*
>
> *Jeremiah 15:10*

The word "curse" in Jeremiah 15:10 means "to make despicable; to curse." Yet when Jeremiah is cursed, the curse had absolutely no power to accomplish anything. In fact, Jeremiah was free while the rest of Israel went into Babylonian captivity (Jeremiah 40:4).

More on Jeremiah:

> *"Cursed <0779> be the day in which I was born! Let the day not be blessed in which my mother bore me! 15 Let the man be cursed <0779> Who brought news to my father, saying, "A male child has been born to you!" Making him very glad. 16 And let that man be like the cities Which the LORD overthrew, and did not relent; Let him hear the cry in the morning And the shouting at noon, 17 Because he did not kill me from the womb, That my mother might have been my grave, And her womb always enlarged with me. 18 Why did I come forth from the womb to see labor and sorrow, That my days should be consumed with shame?"*
>
> *Jeremiah 20:14-18*

Jeremiah cursed himself and the one who brought news that he had been born. Jeremiah's cursing was the heart of a mourning man. There is zero evidence his curse produced anything. The day he was born was already passed. And concerning the man who brought news of his birth, could the curse become retroactive? Furthermore, did the proclamation of this curse actually send a curse the herald's way? The day was in the past; the news was in the past. But if words have power, especially when spoken by a prophet, then time, I suppose, wouldn't matter. God's words aren't time bound. So if man's words can have power like God's do, then these words of Jeremiah would have changed history; he would not have been born. Sounds like fantasy—a fiction movie. And yet, some Christians have theology in line with such a view.

Above are just a few examples, but the same canon is throughout the OT. Often God's people used the negative things spoken to them as a platform for their prayers, as in the Psalms of David and the prayer of Hezekiah. They prayed the opposite of what their enemies said to them— even the curses. Their focus was not on the curse or those who spoke it. It was on God and what He had to say.

New Testament

Very little is discussed in the New Testament about the power of words spoken to God's people, except when using the Name of Jesus in demonstration of the Spirit's power. The NT's emphasis is far different than many in God's family believe and teach. What the NT says on this subject has already been candidly discussed. Therefore, we will look at only a couple sections of scripture for the NT's perspective on the power of words spoken to God's people. These potent scripture sections carry such great weight and clarity that they will, by examination, reveal a very foundational bedrock base for NT believers' theology.

Bless Those Who Curse You

> [Jesus speaking] *"You have heard that it was said, 'You shall love your neighbor and hate your enemy.' 44 But I say to you, love your enemies, bless those who curse you, do good to those who hate you, and pray for those who spitefully use you and persecute you, 45 that you may be sons of your Father in heaven; for He makes His sun rise on the evil and on the good, and sends rain on the just and on the unjust. 46 For if you love those who love you, what reward have you? Do not even the tax collectors do the same? 47 And if you greet your brethren only, what do you do more than others? Do not even the tax collectors do so? 48 Therefore you shall be perfect, just as your Father in heaven is perfect."*
>
> *Matthew 5:43-48*

In Matthew 5:44 Jesus says we are to bless those who curse us—that is the NT response. Why would Jesus say this if there would be a spiritual force released on us by cursing words? He wouldn't. He didn't. Instead, He would have told us to cast off or cast out demons, break off curses, or cancel their words. But He didn't. Regarding this subject, the NT's emphasis is personal responsibility before God. No blame shifting. We are responsible for ourselves: our attitude, our sin, our beliefs, and our character. Some circumstances are beyond our control, such as where we were born, to what family, social status, etc., nevertheless our actions and our attitude are ours to own and control. Consider that many people rejected Jesus. So if words have power to unleash spiritual forces, why did people reject Jesus? How could they resist such power? He was God in the flesh—the Word of God Himself. Wouldn't His word carry more authority to create and destroy than any other? Or how about the prophets who spoke God's very words? If anyone could be bound by words, would it not be God's very word that had the most influential power to control people? Yet, not even one scripture states Jesus let someone off the hook because they were unable to come to Him or follow Him because of another person. Not even for a curse. The Bible is very clear that it is a matter of personal responsibility before God, not the words spoken or the actions of others. Remember the demoniac with Legion? Legion could not stop this man from running to Jesus to worship at His feet. Jesus never says the words or curses of others defile a man. Only one's very own heart—that is what defiles a man.

From Within

And He [Jesus] said, "What comes out of a man, that defiles a man. 21 For from within, out of the heart of men, proceed evil thoughts, adulteries, fornications, murders, 22 thefts, covetousness, wickedness, deceit, lewdness, an evil eye, blasphemy, pride, foolishness. 23 All these evil things come from within and defile a man."

Mark 7:20-23

Note the emphasis is on the speaker. Their words reveal their heart. The speaker is defiled by their own words springing from their own dark heart. That is Jesus' perspective and I think I'll go with Him.

Closing Remarks by God

"Indeed they shall surely assemble, but not because of Me. Whoever assembles against you shall fall for your sake. 16 Behold, I have created the blacksmith Who blows the coals in the fire, Who brings forth an instrument for his work; And I have created the spoiler to destroy. 17 No weapon formed against you shall prosper, And every tongue which rises against you in judgment You shall condemn. This is the heritage of the servants of the LORD, And their righteousness is from Me," Says the LORD.

Isaiah 54:15-17

Isaiah 54's voice pole-vaults into the New Covenant and into the Millennial Age. God is the one who said that no weapon formed against us will prosper, and every tongue which rises against us in judgment we would condemn. He points everything in these scriptures back to Himself and His omnipotence. He created the blacksmith and He purchased our righteousness. Romans 8 so powerfully displays this truth:

> *Who shall bring a charge against God's elect? It is God who justifies. 34 Who is he who condemns? It is Christ who died, and furthermore is also risen, who is even at the right hand of God, who also makes intercession for us. 35 Who shall separate us from the love of Christ? Shall tribulation, or distress, or persecution, or famine, or nakedness, or peril, or sword? 36 As it is written: "For Your sake we are killed all day long; We are accounted as sheep for the slaughter." 37 Yet in all these things we are more than conquerors through Him who loved us.*
>
> *Romans 8:33-37*

What can anyone do to us who are bought with the precious blood of Christ? Even death has lost its victory and sting. Jesus, when standing before Pontus Pilate, the elders, and chief priests, didn't even open His mount in defense (Matthew 27). How did He condemn those who rose up against Him? Through the Cross. Paul in both 2 Corinthians 10 and Ephesians 6 said our weapons are supernatural: our sword is the Word of God and our might is prayer.

Chapter 4

Confessing Scripture

Jesus, God's People, and Satan

A BRIEF DISCUSSION about confession. Many Christians believe they can create when they speak, much like God does when He speaks. They believe this is true especially when they are quoting scriptures. Whole denominations have built a great deal of their foundation upon confession as their biblical worldview: speaking to create their reality. Confessing scripture is biblical. Jesus confessed scripture, God's people confessed scripture, the disciples confessed scripture, and so did the devil. We have probably all heard unbelievers quote scripture too. Sometimes correctly; sometimes not. For example, how many times have we heard an unbeliever say, "It's all for a purpose" or "It will turn out for good"? They are unknowingly referring to Romans 8:28, which is for those who love God and not a broad base foundation for all people. In this chapter we will look briefly at the confession of scripture by Jesus, God's people, and by the devil.

Jesus

Jesus confessed scripture. He quoted the OT when the devil confronted Him. Jesus quoted OT prophecies to bring current events into biblical context and to reveal who He was. He quoted OT scriptures when He taught, and to increase faith in those who heard Him. Jesus also baited the religious by bringing up OT scriptures He knew would surface their hearts. (Mark 12:1-12 is classic.) He never quoted or confessed scripture apart from what the Father was already saying. Jesus heard, then spoke. Jesus never quoted or confessed scripture to create an atmosphere.

Because of Jesus' very nature as God, the only begotten—the Word in flesh—He uniquely was the communication of God to man. Hebrew 1:3 (NASV) states: *And He [Jesus] is the radiance of His [God's] glory and the exact representation of His nature...* Jesus not only confessed scripture, as He spoke, He spoke scripture. Whatever He said or did was Logos. Logos, the Greek word for "Word" in John 1, is Jesus:

> *In the beginning was the Word [Jesus: Logos], and the Word [Jesus: Logos] was with God, and the Word [Jesus: Logos] was God. 2 He was in the beginning with God... 14 And the Word [Jesus: Logos] became flesh and dwelt among us, and we beheld His glory, the glory as of the only begotten of the Father, full of grace and truth.*
>
> *John 1:1-2, 1:14*

Satan

Satan quoted OT scripture out of context. His intent was and is to deceive people. He does this by twisting the scriptures and taking them out of context. Scripture then takes on a meaning God never intended. In the rare occasion when he quotes scripture in context, likely it is to get people to respond impulsively and out of God's timing or to prove something. (For example, Satan told Jesus that he would give Him the kingdoms of this world if Jesus would worship him. Interestingly this "position" of ruling the kingdoms of this world is unique of two people in history: Jesus during the future Millennial Kingdom Age (Psalms 2:8; Revelation 11:15) and the antichrist during the end of this age. The antichrist will take Satan up on the offer Jesus rejected.) Our weapons against such attacks is to know Jesus, tell demons to leave in Jesus' Name, and quote the word of God accurately back to them. Not that we quote the original Greek or Hebrew or any version, rather we get the meaning correct.

God's People

God's people confessed scripture to explain prophetic events' fulfillment, in teaching, and in revealing Jesus as Messiah. His people never confessed scripture to create an atmosphere, to create a reality, or to get what they wanted—unless God spoke it first. Receiving what they spoke was always tied to hearing God first. We confess scripture to build our faith, not to create. And not to make God servant to our words. A scenario for many misguided believers goes something like this: they take a scripture such as: *Delight yourself also in the LORD, And He shall give you the desires of your heart (Psalm 37:4).* Then they confess it over and over in order to claim their desire. Many errors surround this confession based theology. Confession does not make God move on our behalf. Neither does confession bring into reality that which we desire. Confessing scripture can increase our faith. We must be careful that our faith is in God and not in the confession, no matter how repetitively we speak it. Furthermore, when we "claim a scripture" it must be regarding the truth of the scripture, not a scripture pulled out of context—unless it is God breathed rhema in the moment, personally for us. God is all about faith and relationship. He is not a vending machine where we put in a scripture and He outputs our desire. Some claim monetary increase by confessing Jesus' abundant life: *"I have come that they may have life, and that they may have it more abundantly" (John 10:10b).* They assume their understanding is the same as Jesus' understanding of abundant life. When riches don't come abundantly, even though they have sowed their seed of $100 bills, often cynicism settles in, which can lead to distrust towards God and His leaders. Such ideology of the Kingdom is wrong. Confessing scriptures does not equate to manifesting the Kingdom.

Summary

The sons of Sceva used the name of Jesus—it ended very badly for them. They spoke Jesus' name, but without the relationship. This means the use of His name is covenant based and not to be wielded by unbelievers. Hence, apart from a covenant based relationship with God, confession is at best a formula. God is not formulaic; He is all about relationship. As discussed previously, the relationship brings the authority to use His name. His name and His word are not magic or charms; they cannot be wielded at will to get what people want.

Chapter 5

The Author

I FIRST BEGAN THIS STUDY in the late 1990s—some 20 years ago. Since then I have been in many different churches: Assemblies of God, American First Baptist, Vineyards, numerous Non-Denominational Charismatic churches, and Calvary Chapels. I have been to many conferences and talked to many Christians with different backgrounds. Often the subject of curses has come up. Every time it does I ask, "Who is the author of curses in the Bible?" Only 3-1/2 times out of hundreds of conversations has the person I was speaking with answered biblically. Staggering! The 1/2 belongs to someone who almost got it right.

This will likely be an uncomfortable section for many.

God is the author of curses—every one of them.

Revealed in the pages of the Bible, God is clearly the author of curses. Curses, that is, with supernatural power. Man curses for sure, but their curses are only mere words.

God's curses impacted the climates, fruitfulness, wealth, freedom from captivity, the land, the heavens, victory over enemies, and mankind. Curses were ALWAYS judgment for sin. God's authorship is exposed with the first curse in the Bible (Genesis 3), in the Ten Commandments (Exodus 20), in Deuteronomy 27-28, and throughout the Bible.

Old Testament

The Beginning

So the LORD God said to the serpent: "Because you have done this, You are cursed
<0779> more than all cattle, And more than every beast of the field; On your belly you
shall go, And you shall eat dust All the days of your life. 15 And I will put enmity
Between you and the woman, And between your seed and her Seed; He shall bruise
your head, And you shall bruise His heel."

16 To the woman He said: "I will greatly multiply your sorrow and your
conception; In pain you shall bring forth children; Your desire shall be for your
husband, And he shall rule over you."

17 Then to Adam He said, "Because you have heeded the voice of your wife, and
have eaten from the tree of which I commanded you, saying, 'You shall not eat of it':
"Cursed <0779> is the ground for your sake; In toil you shall eat of it All the days of
your life. 18 Both thorns and thistles it shall bring forth for you, And you shall eat the
herb of the field. 19 In the sweat of your face you shall eat bread Till you return to the
ground, For out of it you were taken; For dust you are, And to dust you shall return."

Genesis 3:14-19

This is the Bible's first mention of a curse. God pronounced and imputed
the curse due to Adam and Eve's sin. All creation on earth fell: animals,
mankind, all future generations, climate, land, plants, and even things
beyond mankind's comprehension. Roman 8 says all of creation was
brought into bondage to decay by this sin. In Section 3 we will explore
creational curses in greater detail.

Noah: Genesis 5-9

And he [Lamech, Noah's father] called his name Noah, saying, "This one will comfort
us concerning our work and the toil of our hands, because of the ground which the
LORD has cursed" <0779>.

Genesis 5:29

God authored the ground's curse. He also destroyed all living things
because of the overwhelming wickedness of mankind and the corruption
of all flesh. (Genesis 6 and 7). God directly and actively is responsible for
destroying all living things through the flood. It was judgment for sin.

After the flood the LORD said: *"I will never again curse <07043> the ground for man's sake, although the imagination of man's heart is evil from his youth; nor will I again destroy every living thing as I have done"* (8:21). Then God, looking down the corridor of time, gave the promise of the rainbow as an everlasting covenant (9:16).

Abraham

Due to His friendship with Abraham, God dealt with people according to how they treated Abraham, His friend. God is clearly the author of these curses. In Genesis 27:29: *"Cursed <0779> be everyone who curses <0779> you, And blessed be those who bless you!"* is passed on to Jacob, and subsequently, Israel through Jacob.

> *Now the LORD had said to Abram: "Get out of your country, From your family And from your father's house, To a land that I will show you. 2 I will make you a great nation; I will bless you And make your name great; And you shall be a blessing. 3 I will bless those who bless you, And I will curse <07043> him who curses <07043> you; And in you all the families of the earth shall be blessed."*
>
> *Genesis 12:1-3*

Israel and the Law: Deuteronomy 27 and 28

These two chapters deal extensively with blessings and curses, though only Deuteronomy 28:20 is cited. The Law voiced how God would deal with His people. Most people easily accept that blessings belong to God, however most have difficulty believing God is also the author of curses. Even when scriptures such as Deuteronomy 28:20 are sited, people still have a hard time grasping that God really curses people. They reason it must be the devil. But that is not the testimony of scripture. God is undoubtedly the author of curses — actively and decisively.

> *"The LORD will send on you cursing <03994>, confusion, and rebuke in all that you set your hand to do, until you are destroyed and until you perish quickly, because of the wickedness of your doings in which you have forsaken Me."*
>
> *Deuteronomy 28:20*

God to Solomon

This is one of the most prominent OT scriptures displaying the wide-ranging ramifications imposed by God according to the behavior of His people. Deuteronomy's blessings and curses are easily seen in 2 Chronicles 7:12-14:

> Then the LORD appeared to Solomon by night, and said to him: "I have heard your prayer, and have chosen this place for Myself as a house of sacrifice. 13 When I shut up heaven and there is no rain, or command the locusts to devour the land, or send pestilence among My people, 14 if My people who are called by My name will humble themselves, and pray and seek My face, and turn from their wicked ways, then I will hear from heaven, and will forgive their sin and heal their land.
>
> *2 Chronicles 7:12-14*

Consider the kindness of God: if His people were experiencing the curses of Deuteronomy 27 and 28, and yet, would turn from their wicked ways, then God would forgive their sin and heal their land. The Jews weren't the only people impacted by their sin or obedience to God. Other people in the land would also reap the benefits, as well as the curses.

Living Deuteronomy 28

In Deuteronomy 28 God is clear what He would do to His people, if they chose to live as they did in Judges 2. Yes, God Himself would send a curse upon His people. Judges 2 is an example of God's curse:

> Then the children of Israel did evil in the sight of the LORD, and served the Baals; 12 and they forsook the LORD God of their fathers, who had brought them out of the land of Egypt; and they followed other gods from among the gods of the people who were all around them, and they bowed down to them; and they provoked the LORD to anger. 13 They forsook the LORD and served Baal and the Ashtoreths. 14 And the anger of the LORD was hot against Israel. So He delivered them into the hands of plunderers who despoiled them; and He sold them into the hands of their enemies all around, so that they could no longer stand before their enemies. 15 Wherever they went out, the hand of the LORD was against them for calamity, as the LORD had said, and as the LORD had sworn to them. And they were greatly distressed. 16 Nevertheless, the LORD raised up judges who delivered them out of the hand of those who plundered them. 17 Yet they would not listen to their judges, but they played the harlot with

other gods, and bowed down to them. They turned quickly from the way in which their fathers walked, in obeying the commandments of the LORD; they did not do so. 18 And when the LORD raised up judges for them, the LORD was with the judge and delivered them out of the hand of their enemies all the days of the judge; for the LORD was moved to pity by their groaning because of those who oppressed them and harassed them. 19 And it came to pass, when the judge was dead, that they reverted and behaved more corruptly than their fathers, by following other gods, to serve them and bow down to them. They did not cease from their own doings nor from their stubborn way. 20 Then the anger of the LORD was hot against Israel; and He said, "Because this nation has transgressed My covenant which I commanded their fathers, and has not heeded My voice, 21 I also will no longer drive out before them any of the nations which Joshua left when he died, 22 so that through them I may test Israel, whether they will keep the ways of the LORD, to walk in them as their fathers kept them, or not. 23 Therefore the LORD left those nations, without driving them out immediately; nor did He deliver them into the hand of Joshua.

Judges 2:11-23

Painful even to read.

Again the children of Israel did evil in the sight of the LORD, and the LORD delivered them into the hand of the Philistines for forty years (Judges 13:1). God used the Philistines to work out His purpose: to discipline and judge His people for 40 years. He is sovereign and everything is at His disposal, even His enemies for His purposes. The Assyrians and Babylonians were also used for God's purpose to discipline His people. The Assyrians invaded the northern kingdom in the 700s BC, conquered them, and took them captive; Judah, the southern kingdom, was led into Babylonian captivity during the ministry of Jeremiah.

Jeremiah 44 is a classic example of God sending His prophet to His rebellious people. Judah said they had obeyed, but hadn't, thus their circumstances became worse. Judah claimed their worsening circumstances were because they stopped serving the queen of heaven, but in truth, it was because the LORD was working against them. Not having fully turned to Him, coupled with their full rejection of His words, His prophet, and proclaiming they would serve the queen of heaven, God judged them. Listen to the word of the LORD to His people, Judah, in Egypt:

Then all the men who knew that their wives had burned incense to other gods, with all the women who stood by, a great multitude, and all the people who dwelt in the land of Egypt, in Pathros, answered Jeremiah, saying: 16 "As for the word that you have spoken to us in the name of the LORD, we will not listen to you! 17 But we will certainly do whatever has gone out of our own mouth, to burn incense to the queen of heaven and pour out drink offerings to her, as we have done, we and our fathers, our kings and our princes, in the cities of Judah and in the streets of Jerusalem. For then we had plenty of food, were well-off, and saw no trouble. 18 But since we stopped burning incense to the queen of heaven and pouring out drink offerings to her, we have lacked everything and have been consumed by the sword and by famine."

Jeremiah 44:15-18

Verse 17 is such an intense tragedy. Their own hearts are revealed in their words. Never really turning to the LORD in their hearts they left a door open for deception. And then misevaluating their circumstances propelled that deception. God's response in verses 26-28:

"Therefore hear the word of the LORD, all Judah who dwell in the land of Egypt: 'Behold, I have sworn by My great name,' says the LORD, 'that My name shall no more be named in the mouth of any man of Judah in all the land of Egypt, saying, "The Lord GOD lives." 27 'Behold, I will watch over them for adversity and not for good. And all the men of Judah who are in the land of Egypt shall be consumed by the sword and by famine, until there is an end to them. 28 'Yet a small number who escape the sword shall return from the land of Egypt to the land of Judah; and all the remnant of Judah, who have gone to the land of Egypt to dwell there, shall know whose words will stand, Mine or theirs."

Jeremiah 44:26-28

Once again echoing the previous pages of this book—God's words—His alone—will stand. No matter how many time these Judeans would confess their devotion and determination to serve the "queen," the Lord would have none of it. They became the tail and not the head, as God said in Deuteronomy 28. Their destruction was eminent.

Lamentations

After Jerusalem was captured by Babylon and led into captivity Jeremiah wrote the book of Lamentations; the result of a curse by God—living Deuteronomy 28. Even though the phrase "a curse by God" is not stated, it is clearly the portrait in Deuteronomy 28. Jerusalem's idolatry and her rebellion against God plunged the princess into slavery. Jeremiah laments over the beloved city in Jerusalem's elegy. Pay attention to God's role as you read Jerusalem's demise. Following are excerpts from the Jeremiah's lament over Jerusalem:

Chapter 1

How lonely sits the city [Jerusalem] That was full of people! How like a widow is she, Who was great among the nations! The princess among the provinces Has become a slave! 2 She weeps bitterly in the night, Her tears are on her cheeks; Among all her lovers She has none to comfort her. All her friends have dealt treacherously with her; They have become her enemies. ...5 Her adversaries have become the master, Her enemies prosper; For the LORD has afflicted her Because of the multitude of her transgressions. Her children have gone into captivity before the enemy. ...14 "The yoke of my transgressions was bound; They were woven together by His hands, And thrust upon my neck. He made my strength fail; The Lord delivered me into the hands of those whom I am not able to withstand." ...21 "They have heard that I sigh, But no one comforts me. All my enemies have heard of my trouble; They are glad that You have done it. Bring on the day You have announced, That they may become like me."

Chapter 2

Standing like an enemy, He has bent His bow; With His right hand, like an adversary, He has slain all who were pleasing to His eye; On the tent of the daughter of Zion, He has poured out His fury like fire. 5 The Lord was like an enemy. He has swallowed up Israel, He has swallowed up all her palaces; He has destroyed her strongholds, And has increased mourning and lamentation In the daughter of Judah. 6 He has done violence to His tabernacle, As if it were a garden; He has destroyed His place of assembly; The LORD has caused The appointed feasts and Sabbaths to be forgotten in Zion. In His burning indignation He has spurned the king and the priest. 7 The Lord has spurned His altar, He has abandoned His sanctuary; He has given up the walls of her palaces Into the hand of the enemy. They have made a noise in the house of the LORD As on the day of a set feast. 8 The LORD has purposed to destroy The wall of the daughter of Zion. He has stretched out a line; He has not withdrawn His hand from destroying; Therefore He has caused the rampart and wall to lament; They languished together. ...17 The LORD has done what He purposed; He has fulfilled His word Which He commanded in days of old. He has thrown down and has not pitied, And He has caused an enemy to rejoice over you; He has exalted the horn of your adversaries.

Chapter 3

7 He has hedged me in so that I cannot get out; He has made my chain heavy. 8 Even when I cry and shout, He shuts out my prayer. 9 He has blocked my ways with hewn stone; He has made my paths crooked. 10 He has been to me a bear lying in wait, Like a lion in ambush. 11 He has turned aside my ways and torn me in pieces; He has made me desolate. 12 He has bent His bow And set me up as a target for the arrow. 13 He has caused the arrows of His quiver To pierce my loins. 14 I have become the ridicule of all my people — Their taunting song all the day. 15 He has filled me with bitterness, He has made me drink wormwood. 16 He has also broken my teeth with gravel, And covered me with ashes. 17 You have moved my soul far from peace; I have forgotten prosperity. 18 And I said, "My strength and my hope Have perished from the LORD." ...37 Who is he who speaks and it comes to pass, When the Lord has not commanded it? 38 Is it not from the mouth of the Most High That woe and well-being proceed?

Excerpts from Lamentations 1-3

As we read through the OT we see God and God alone led Judah and Israel into captivity. He used the Babylonians and the Assyrians in His cause—nations more wicked than themselves. In Lamentations we touch the heartbroken prophet's pain as we read of the beloved city's ruin. Recalling from the depths of Deuteronomy 28: *"Now it shall come to pass, if you diligently obey the voice of the LORD your God, to observe carefully all His commandments which I command you today, that the LORD your God will set you high above all nations of the earth (28:1) [and you will be blessed].* But Jerusalem didn't obey. And He, as Lamentations states, became their enemy. He fought against them, the Babylonians were His weapon. God clearly does not delight in afflicting His people (Lamentations 3:33), but He does so for the ultimate good—to turn people to righteousness. Verses 3:37-38 again emphasize that God is the Sovereign; it is He who speaks and it comes to pass: *"Who is he who speaks and it comes to pass, When the Lord has not commanded it? 38 Is it not from the mouth of the Most High That woe and well-being proceed?"*

Haggai to Zerubbabel and Joshua

Haggai's prophesied repentance. Just as God had detailed in Deuteronomy, the Israelite's sin penetrated the land, man, climate, animals, finances, and harvest. Repentance was their only solution:

In the second year of King Darius, in the sixth month, on the first day of the month, the word of the LORD came by Haggai the prophet to Zerubbabel the son of Shealtiel, governor of Judah, and to Joshua the son of Jehozadak, the high priest, saying, 2 "Thus speaks the LORD of hosts, saying: 'This people says, "The time has not come, the time that the LORD's house should be built."'" 3 Then the word of the LORD came by Haggai the prophet, saying, 4 "Is it time for you yourselves to dwell in your paneled houses, and this temple to lie in ruins?" 5 Now therefore, thus says the LORD of hosts: "Consider your ways! 6 You have sown much, and bring in little; You eat, but do not have enough; You drink, but you are not filled with drink; You clothe yourselves, but no one is warm; And he who earns wages, Earns wages to put into a bag with holes." 7 Thus says the LORD of hosts: "Consider your ways! 8 Go up to the mountains and bring wood and build the temple, that I may take pleasure in it and be glorified," says the LORD. 9 "You looked for much, but indeed it came to little; and when you brought it home, I blew it away. Why?" says the LORD of hosts. "Because of My house that is in ruins, while every one of you runs to his own house. 10 Therefore the heavens above you withhold the dew, and the earth withholds its fruit. 11 For I called for a drought on the land and the mountains, on the grain and the new wine and the oil, on whatever the ground brings forth, on men and livestock, and on all the labor of your hands."...12 Then Zerubbabel the son of Shealtiel, and Joshua the son of Jehozadak, the high priest, with all the remnant of the people, obeyed the voice of the LORD their God, and the words of Haggai the prophet, as the LORD their God had sent him; and the people feared the presence of the LORD. 13 Then Haggai, the LORD'S messenger, spoke the LORD'S message to the people, saying, "I am with you, says the LORD."

Haggai 1

God was the source of the Israelites' problems and He was their solution. Verse 9 states that God blew away what they brought home and verse 11 states that He called for the drought. They were living a curse, but didn't realize it until the prophet Haggai came with the word of the LORD.

God, the Author of OT Curses

Many scriptures reverberate this same bellowing from deep within the pages of the Bible: God alone is the author of curses. God clearly penned the blessings and curses in Deuteronomy; they are stated first person. Psalm 106 is an overview of the children of Israel's relationship to God and His dealings with them: when they served the LORD they were blessed and when they turn against Him He raised His hand against them (:26). Interestingly, the last OT scripture is: *"And he [Elijah to come]* *will turn The hearts of the fathers to the children, And the hearts of the children to their fathers, Lest I [God] come and strike the earth with a curse <02764>"* (Malachi 4:6).

But that was life under the Old Covenant. What about living under the New Covenant in His Blood? Have things changed? In the next chapter we systematically study the NT scriptures in view of curses and life in the New Covenant.

Chapter 6

What's My Problem Then?

Living in the New Covenant

Keep in mind the NT, from Romans through Revelation, is written to churches and to Christians by its One, though various, author. The NT has very little to say about curses, with the exception of Galatians 3. We must form doctrine based on what the NT does say, while working through its thunderous silence on curses. What the Bible says is base aggregate. How we put the scriptures together is our structure: our building (1 Corinthians 3). The NT's focus is on what Jesus did and what the Holy Spirit is doing. This includes the church—God's redeemed covenant people, faith, preaching of the Gospel, God's power, repentance, salvation, authority, the heart of man, the coming judgment, God's ultimate plan, and the now and yet to come Kingdom of God.

Recall from previous chapters, man's words, in themselves, do not have spiritual power. God's words have spiritual power. Man's words only have spiritual power when they are agreeing with what He is saying or has said, and therefore the words are, in truth, God's words and not man's. Under the Old Covenant, curses were imputed and propelled by God as judgment for sin. The intent was to bring people to repentance. If they would not repent worse judgment followed. Now, since God is the author of the curses, what role could curses possibly play in the life of a child of God? We are His purchased possession redeemed by His blood: *He has delivered us from the power of darkness and conveyed us into the kingdom of the Son of His love, 14 in whom we have redemption through His blood, the forgiveness of sins (Colossians 1:13-14).* Jesus set aside God's wrath, which on account of our sin was due us, through His death on the Cross. Jesus took upon Himself our owed penalty: our judgment. However, in the Book of Revelation we will see there still is more to say on curses from a New Testament viewpoint.

Curses in View of New Covenant Theology

Jesus Became a Curse for Us

Galatians 3 is the most prominent reference to curses in the NT. Verse 10 overshadows those under the Old Covenant Law. It sadly states: *For as many as are of the works of the law are under the curse.* Paul argues with great clarity the case against those under law verses those in Christ. We can easily imagine Paul standing in front of a court arguing that those under law are under the curse, whereas those in Christ are blessed. Hear his case:

> *For as many as are of the works of the law are under the curse <2671>; for it is written, "Cursed <1944> is everyone who does not continue in all things which are written in the book of the law, to do them." 11 But that no one is justified by the law in the sight of God is evident, for "the just shall live by faith." 12 Yet the law is not of faith, but "the man who does them shall live by them." 13 Christ has redeemed us from the curse <2671> of the law, having become a curse <2671> for us (for it is written, "Cursed <1944> is everyone who hangs on a tree"), 14 that the blessing of Abraham might come upon the Gentiles in Christ Jesus, that we might receive the promise of the Spirit through faith.*
>
> *Galatians 3:10-14*

Galatians 3 without doubt states that Jesus Christ became a curse for us by hanging on the Cross—the very same place He became sin for us. Just as He became the sin offering to purchase our forgiveness and righteousness, so too, He became a curse to set us free from the curse of the law that bound every man, woman, and child to judgment. Curses were ALWAYS authored by God and were ALWAYS judgment for sin. On the Cross Jesus Christ paid our debt to the law and to God. Recollect from Deuteronomy the severe penalties for not abiding by the law's requirements. The truth being that no one could. The Law required complete unerring obedience. No partial compliance was sufficient or acceptable. Hence, the curse of the law overshadowed all people. When Jesus Christ paid the price on the Cross, He paid it in full once for all. As His sacrifice paid for the forgiveness of sins, so too, it paid for the termination of all curses.

> *And you, being dead in your trespasses and the uncircumcision of your flesh, He has made alive together with Him, having forgiven you all trespasses, 14 having wiped out the handwriting of requirements (the law) that was against us, which was contrary to us. And He has taken it out of the way, having nailed it to the cross.*
>
> *Colossians 2:13-14*

If the Cross of Christ set us free from sin and death, then, undoubtedly, curses were also nailed to the Cross in Him. It must be so, for we cannot have one without the other.

A New Creation in Christ

> *Therefore, if anyone is in Christ, he is a new creation; old things have passed away; behold, all things have become new.*
>
> *2 Corinthians 5:17*

The word "creation" is from the Greek verb ktizo [to create]. It is tied to God's Genesis 1 seven days of creation. When someone receives Christ they become a new creation—the old is past, the new has come. The problem therefore is not our standing with God, rather with our mindsets; our beliefs; our thinking. Our mindset survived the Cross. We must daily renew our minds to align with holiness and righteousness. Ephesians puts it this way:

> *...that you put off, concerning your former conduct, the old man which grows corrupt according to the deceitful lusts, 2 and be renewed in the spirit of your mind, 24 and that you put on the new man which was created according to God, in true righteousness and holiness.*
>
> *Ephesians 4:22-24*

The umbilical cord to the past is severed: we are free. Now we must learn to walk in our freedom. Renewing our minds so that we think, believe, and act as God intends is the goal.

Paul in Athens and Ephesus

> *Now while Paul waited for them at Athens, his spirit was provoked within him when he saw that the city was given over to idols. 17 Therefore he reasoned in the synagogue with the Jews and with the Gentile worshipers, and in the marketplace daily with those who happened to be there.*
>
> Acts 17:16-17

1 Corinthians 10 reveals demons are involved in idol worship: *What am I saying then? That an idol is anything, or what is offered to idols is anything? 20 Rather, that the things which the Gentiles sacrifice they sacrifice to demons and not to God, and I do not want you to have fellowship with demons (1 Corinthians 10:19-20).* Demons were a large part of the culture in Athens. The full Biblical account of Paul's stay in Athens discloses he preached the Gospel starting with the creation, brought in hope for their existence, revealed God as personable, that God expects all men to repent, declared Jesus as the One, and then ended with the Judgment and the Resurrection. However, Paul doesn't address curses, instead the Bible says he reasoned with the people. Interesting. Even in Athens, full of idols, there was no mention of curses. It obviously was not part of Paul's theology. I guess he thought the Gospel was enough to set people free. After all it is the power of God to salvation for those who believe, as stated in Romans 1:16. If not in Athens, how about in Ephesus, a place full of magic, were curses mentioned?

Following demons attacking the sons of Sceva, and subsequently many seeing the power of God in the Name of Jesus, Acts 19 continues:

> *And many who had believed came confessing and telling their deeds. 19 Also, many of those who had practiced magic brought their books together and burned them in the sight of all. And they counted up the value of them, and it totaled fifty thousand pieces of silver. 20 So the word of the Lord grew mightily and prevailed.*
>
> Acts 19:18-20

Paul spent three years in Ephesus. First in the *synagogue [he] spoke boldly for three months, reasoning and persuading concerning the things of the kingdom of God.* Then for two years Paul reasoned in the School of Tyrannus. All Asia heard the word during those two years (19:10). In Ephesus there were idols, people practicing magic, and demons, but breaking curses is not mentioned. We can see that the people repented, since they burned their costly magic paraphernalia. And yet, it was the preaching of the Gospel that Acts mentions and not breaking curses. With the abundance of idolatry, magic, and demons in Ephesus, if curses were even on the radar shouldn't they at least be mentioned? But there isn't even a hint of curses. The Gospel and preaching the word was enough. Is it for you?

The Epistles

In the previous section, the scriptures deal with salvation and those first coming to Christ. But what about us, we who are in Christ, but haven't gained victory in all areas of our lives? Could curses be the reason?

In the NT curses are never the reason Christians sin. Instead, the NT says the problem is sin and worldliness already existing within us. Paul, in 1 Thessalonians 4:3, states to the Thessalonian believers: *For this is the will of God, your sanctification…* We are saved; we are indwelt by the Holy Spirit, we are sanctified (Hebrews 10:10), but we still need sanctification (Hebrews 10:14). Jesus says it is out of our own hearts that the vilest of evils flow. The NT's remedy is never to break a curse or cast a demon out of a Christian. Not even one time. The answer the NT gives is quite different. First, consider that people, regarding sin, are dealing with three issues: the power of sin, the penalty for sin, and the desire for sin. The penalty for sin was paid by Jesus Christ on the Cross. We freely receive forgiveness and justification when we are born again. The power of sin and the desire for sin are tied together. They fluctuate depending upon us—what we feed on—that is, what we allow in our minds.

We would all agree that Jesus Christ's sacrifice delivers us from the penalty of sin. The power of sin is fed by our desire for sin. The more desire is fed, the greater the power of sin in our lives. If we starve the desire for sin, the power of sin weakens and loses its strength. Galatians 5:16 ties our relationship with the Holy Spirit directly to our ability to not carry out the desires of the flesh: *Walk in the Spirit, and you shall not fulfill the lust of the flesh.* Lusts are still alive in us, but by walking in the Spirit we will not fulfill them. Walking in the Spirit isn't easy and that is why some look for an easier way out, but there just isn't one.

Romans has references containing the subjunctive mood; it renders the potential and possibility for completing an action and not a demand of such an action. For example, Romans 6:4 states that since we died with Christ in baptism, and were raised with Him in newness of life that: *"we also should* <subjunctive mood> *walk in newness of life."* We choose. We may walk in newness of life, we should walk in newness of life, but we may not walk in newness of life. Thus, personal responsibility is ignited.

Let's look at Paul's magnum opus. Our focus will begin with Romans 6, since it captures the NT's theme regarding our problem with sin. Personal responsibility is at the heart of Paul's penning. And if personal responsibility, we dare not blame shift to anything else, not even a curse.

Romans: Paul's Magnum Opus

Romans 6

> *...knowing this, that our old man was crucified with Him, that the body of sin might* <subjunctive mood> *be done away with, that we should no longer be slaves of sin. 7 For he who has died has been freed from sin.*
>
> Romans 6:6-7

This is the paradox: we are crucified with Christ, we, therefore, are no longer slaves to sin through Christ Jesus, but we can still serve sin, if we choose to do so. Howbeit, we should not. For how can we who died to sin live to serve sin? Curses are understood, in many Christian circles, to have a supernatural grip on people. An invisible claim to keep them bound by forces unilluminated, shrouded in mystery, needing revelation in order to be broken. That is not NT theology. Christianity is much simpler and much harder.

Look at verses 11-18. Note the prominent terminology (dominion, reign, slaves, and obey) are all pointing to a king and a kingdom, with verse 16 as the keynote speaker. Pay attention to the commands "consider" and "do not." They denote personal responsibility. Additionally, this text is filled with both the imperative mood[1] and the indicative[2] mood:

> *Likewise you also, reckon[1] yourselves* [personal; responsibility] *to be dead indeed to sin, but alive to God in Christ Jesus our Lord. 12 Therefore do not* [command] *let sin reign in your mortal body, that you should obey it in its lusts* [if you obey it, it is your king]. *13 And do not* [command: personal responsibility] *present[1] your members as instruments of unrighteousness to sin, but present yourselves to God* [command: personal responsibility] *as being alive from the dead, and your members as instruments of righteousness to God. 14 For sin shall not have dominion[2]* [have dominion, be lord] *over you, for you are[2] not under law but under grace. 15 What then? Shall we sin because we are not under law but under grace* [presenting the choice]*? Certainly not[3]! 16 Do you not know that to whom you present[2] yourselves* [choice] *slaves to obey, you are[2] that one's slaves whom you obey[2], whether of sin leading to death, or of obedience leading to righteousness?* [Note the choice presented; the thought continues…] *17 But God be thanked that though you were[2] slaves of sin, yet you obeyed[2] from the heart that form of doctrine* [obedience to teaching led to freedom] *to which you were delivered. 18 And having been set free from sin* [by choosing to obey]*, you became slaves of righteousness* [by choosing obedience to righteousness]*. 19 I speak in human terms because of the weakness of your flesh. For just as you presented[2] your members as slaves of uncleanness, and of lawlessness leading to more lawlessness, so now present[1]* [a command: a choice] *your members as slaves of righteousness for holiness.*
>
> Romans 6:11-19

God created humans with free will. The Fall made us slaves to sin. Sin then became our master. The Law was added because of transgressions. Christ died to set us free. In Him, legally, we are free from sin. The prison door is open, but we choose whether we live in freedom. Sin reigning in a

---

[1] Imperative: the imperative mood corresponds to the English imperative, and expresses a command to the hearer to perform a certain action by the order and authority of the one commanding.

[2] Indicative: the indicative mood is a simple statement of fact. If an action really occurs or has occurred or will occur, it will be rendered in the indicative mood.

[3] Optative: the optative mood is generally used in the so-called "fourth-class" conditions which express a wish or desire for an action to occur in which the completion of such is doubtful.

Christian is an oxymoron. We must not allow its reign.

As we see in verse 19, walking in righteousness is commanded. If it were natural for a Christian to live righteously, why would it be commanded? Paul, by the Holy Spirit, would offer different terminology, wouldn't he? But here, as in the bulk of the NT, it is commanded. And if commanded, then it renders that it is not, at least early on, a natural flow from the new life. Even when we want to please God, worldly left-overs from our pre-Christ life lure us towards sin: habits, mindsets, temptation, and the sway of evil in the world are all at work.

Romans 7

Before we start Romans 7 it is important to discuss two views on Romans 7. Is Paul speaking of his life pre or post conversion? Commentators divide on both sides. One thing we can all agree on is the struggle with sin Paul discusses in Romans 7. A struggle prominent in many epistles: how do we overcome and live to please God? Furthermore, anyone who sees Romans 7 as Paul's pre-cross should pause and consider their own life. Why do they still struggle with sin? Why haven't they overcome in all areas of their life? Is Romans 7 more pertinent than first thought? For though we are born again we are still prone to sin, even though we have been set free. Isn't that the paradox? Free, yet working out our freedom? The language in Romans 7 is present tense: Paul bellows: *"O wretched man that I am!"*

Romans juxtaposes freedom and Law. Law bypasses freedom. And yet, some Christians keep living under law. Legalism kills heart; it gives an incredible strength to sin; it is a façade and it has no ability to change the heart. Whichever side we end on concerning Romans 7, Paul's pre-conversion or post, one conclusion is certain: it is not the breaking of a curse that sets one free: *[For] Who will deliver me from this body of death? I thank God — through Jesus Christ our Lord! (Romans 7:24-25).*

Romans 8

The flow of thought in Romans 8:

- Since we are in Christ we are not under condemnation and Law.
- Christ did what Law could not do—He condemned sin in the flesh.
- Now we live according to another law—the law of the Spirit of life.
- We are in the Spirit not in the flesh.
- Since we are in the Spirit, we are to live according to the Spirit.
- We are to renew, rewire, and renovate what goes on in our mind.

It would be so much easier if God would just do a hard reset, but instead we must set our minds on what the Spirit desires with the help of God. Really, truth be told, how well we renew our mind will determine how successfully we live as Christians. Our whole life, up to the point we received Jesus, we were in the flesh. Setting our minds on what the flesh desired: what it dictated. We have a lot of re-wiring to do. Thank God, through Jesus Christ, He helps and enables us. Notice, though, how Romans 8 doesn't say that we automatically get a factory reboot. We have to work with the Lord to delete and write-over files in our head. 2 Corinthians 10:3-5 says that forcing our thoughts to obey Christ it is spiritual warfare. Also, we are told to work out our own salvation with fear and trembling (Philippians 2:12). No wonder it is so difficult at times. Romans 8 so clearly sets the record straight regarding our choices:

Therefore, brethren, we are debtors — not to the flesh, to live according to the flesh. 13 For if you live according to the flesh you will die; but if by the Spirit you put to death the deeds of the body, you will live. 14 For as many as are led by the Spirit of God, these are sons of God.

Romans 8:12-14

Recall Romans is written: *To all who are in Rome, beloved of God, called to be saints (Romans 1:7).* These saints of God were under no obligation [one who owes another, a debtor] to the flesh. No obligation to a curse. Who could bind one whom the Spirit has set free? Yet, these saints are told, if... *if by the Spirit*...they put to death the deeds of the body—rendering their choice to whom they will serve:

What then shall we say to these things? If God is for us, who can be against us? 32 He who did not spare His own Son, but delivered Him up for us all, how shall He not with Him also freely give us all things? 33 Who shall bring a charge against God's elect? It is God who justifies. 34 Who is he who condemns? It is Christ who died, and furthermore is also risen, who is even at the right hand of God, who also makes intercession for us.

Romans 8:31-34

All this Jesus Christ has done for us. Recall curses were always God's judgment for sin. Jesus Christ paid for our sin in full. How could this God bring judgment for sin upon us when: *He who did not spare His own Son, but delivered Him up for us all, how shall He not with Him also freely give us all things? (8:32)*. Consider that if curses still exist in a Christian's life, then Christ died in vain and judgement still looms over our lives. Therefore, anyone who believes in curses in/on a Christian is believing a lie. Very sad when the payment is so very glorious.

Snapshots from the Epistles

Following are highlights from a few of the remaining epistles. To reiterate, the NT does not even make a hint at breaking curses. Curses were not a topic of discussion in the NT churches. The language of the epistles is living by the Holy Spirit and personal responsibility before God: put off the old man and put on the new, because you are now a child of God, empowered by His Spirit. As children of God, sanctification is both inherent (by the Holy Spirit) and to be worked out by us. The Holy Spirit works in us, but He also works with us. Following are epistolary examples where personal responsibility was expected:

- In Corinth a man was fornicating with his stepmother. He was expected to repent. He was not delivered from a curse or a demon. The church expelled him so he would come to his senses and repent. He did and was restored.

- Galatians: Paul candidly rebukes Peter in front of the other leaders due to his duplicity. Additionally, Paul was astonished at the Galatians' retreating from living by the Spirit and going back to law: *Are you so foolish? Having begun in the Spirit, are you now being made perfect by the flesh? (Galatians 3:3)*. This theme is carried throughout the book.

- In Ephesians, Paul implores the saints to walk worthy of their calling with godly character. He states it is through the ministry of the 5-fold (apostles, prophets, evangelists, pastors, and teachers), by the church

87

speaking the truth in love, and ministering to one another that they grow up (Ephesians 4:11-16). They were also given precise instructions on how to behave as believers and how to be imitators of God. Clearly they needed to be taught what that meant.

- Philippians continues: *Only let your conduct be worthy of the gospel of Christ... (1:27).* How Jesus lived in action and attitude is how we are supposed to live too: *Let this mind be in you which was also in Christ Jesus... [He] made Himself of no reputation, taking the form of a bondservant... He humbled Himself and became obedient... (2:5-8).* Paul lingers in his thinking: *... work out your own salvation with fear and trembling; for it is God who works in you both to will and to do for His good pleasure (2:12-13).* And then pens this magnificent bravura: *Not that I have already attained, or am already perfected; but I press on, that I may lay hold of that for which Christ Jesus has also laid hold of me (3:12).*

- For Colossae Paul prayed that they would be filled with the knowledge of God's will in all spiritual wisdom and understanding, so that they would walk in a manner worthy of the Lord, pleasing Him in all respects. Note Paul's heart: *Him we preach, warning every man and teaching every man in all wisdom, that we may present every man perfect in Christ Jesus (1:28).* It was through teaching, not breaking a curse, they would mature.

- The Thessalonians: *...how [they] turned to God from idols to serve a living and true God (1 Thessalonians 1:9).* They turned. Remember demons are attached to idols and yet no there isn't a mention of deliverance from demons or curses. Instead, Paul says he encouraged and implored them as a father would his own children, to walk in a manner worthy of the God (2:12).

We could go through every epistle, but will instead end this section with a brief discussion on Revelation 2 and 3.

Revelation 2 and 3: Personal Responsibility

Revelation 2 and 3 are composed of seven letters, written to seven churches, as dictated by Jesus to the Apostle John. Each of them a personal analysis of the church from God's perspective. Two of the churches were without correction and five were given the ultimatum: repent or else. Jesus never allowed an excuse from these churches. His only remedy was "repent." Even Thyatira and Pergamum, cities where Satan's involvement was clear, the remedy was still to repent. In Smyrna, Satan is also mentioned, yet this church is without correction. Satan is powerful, and yes, he does cause trouble, persecution, and even death, but he is no match for God. God's answer, even in these satanic infested places, was to repent.

Summary

Not one example of a curse being broken by a person is found in the NT. It is foreign to NT teaching. NT doctrine aligns with Acts 10:38: *"…how God anointed Jesus of Nazareth with the Holy Spirit and with power, who went about doing good and healing all who were oppressed by the devil, for God was with Him."* Jesus only broke a curse one time: when He hung on the Cross and became that curse. Jesus exemplified what He commands us to do: *"And as you go, preach, saying, 'The kingdom of heaven is at hand.' 8 Heal the sick, cleanse the lepers, raise the dead, cast out demons. Freely you have received, freely give"* (Matthew 10:7-8). People were healed because of faith, not because a curse was broken off of them. Our testimony should be the same as the author of Hebrews: *"The LORD is my helper; I will not fear. What can man do to me?"* (Hebrews 13:6). Would the author say this if a curse could be pronounced on us by another? No.

Chapter 7

Last Considerations

Curses and the Unbeliever

P EOPLE HAVE ASKED ME WHETHER or not I believed a curse can be put on an unbeliever by a Satanist. They have asked using multiple terms and ideas such as magic, sorcery, occult practices, etc. Boiling it down it all leads to Satan and demons. In the spirit realm, besides God and angels (who are God's servants), apart from our own human self, the devil and his demons are who we deal with. Therefore, for the unbeliever, on a spiritual level, if it isn't other people or their words, and if it isn't God, then it is demonic spirits behind the spiritual veil. And yet, even as I consider the intense ramifications the demonic realm brings, it isn't my concern for the unbelievers anyway. My concern for the unbeliever is that they are under God's law of sin and death already. A loving God is both their problem and their solution.

As we study 2 Thessalonians below, pay attention to these identities mentioned and their role: the devil, people, the lawless man, and God. Pause at verses 11 and 12; reread them, and then, reread them again. God is intense.

Let no one deceive you by any means; for that Day [the day of Christ (2:2)] will not come unless the falling away comes first, and the man of sin is revealed, the son of perdition, 4 who opposes and exalts himself above all that is called God or that is worshiped, so that he sits as God in the temple of God, showing himself that he is God. 5 Do you not remember that when I was still with you I told you these things? 6 And now you know what is restraining, that he may be revealed in his own time. 7 For the mystery of lawlessness is already at work; only He who now restrains will do so until He is taken out of the way. 8 And then the lawless one will be revealed, whom the Lord will consume with the breath of His mouth and destroy with the brightness of His coming. 9 The coming of the lawless one is according to the working of Satan, with all power, signs, and lying wonders, 10 and with all unrighteous deception among those who perish, because they did not receive the love of the truth, that they might be saved. 11 And for this reason God will send them strong delusion, that they should believe the lie, 12 that they all may be condemned who did not believe the truth but had pleasure in unrighteousness.

2 Thessalonians 2:3-12

Note, God *will send them strong delusion, that they should believe the lie (2:11)*. That is incredibly intense. The word "strong" <1753> is an interesting word; "in the NT used only of superhuman power, whether of God or of the Devil."

There are two people mentioned as coming: the Lord and the man of sin, whose activity is according to Satan. At that time (meaning a specific time: verse 6) there are people who are determined to resist God. They serve this lawless man whose activity is according to the superhuman <1753> power of Satan. Through his power this lawless one preforms signs and false wonders with all deception of wickedness. Deception of wickedness through signs and false wonders leading to deception, to those who did not love the truth. Note God—yes God—will send upon them a supernatural influence <1753>, so that they will believe what is false in order that they may be judged, because they did not love the truth. These are very strong words.

Now let's journey into Revelation, where we will look at Jesus, the Seals, Bowls, Trumpets, and Woes.

Revelation 4 vectors the book into a new direction. Chapter 4 begins with John standing before an open door in heaven, and a voice saying: *"Come up here, and I will show you things which must take place after this."* Chapter 5 introduces the seven seals. Jesus Christ Himself takes the book (scroll) with the seals from the right hand of Him who sits on the Throne—for He is worthy! He then, as chapter 6 unfolds, opens each seal one by one, releasing the judgments contained within upon the antichrist and his kingdom. The seventh and final seal seems to contain all that further leads up to the return of Jesus Christ—the trumpets, the bowls, and the woes. This is all at the hands of our Lord Jesus.

Herein lies the question: are the seals that Jesus opens curses upon this lawless man, who people call the antichrist, and those who obstinately harden their hearts towards God? 2 Thessalonians and Revelation are, I believe, discussing the same period of time. The broken seals sound like extreme executions of the curses in Deuteronomy (and Zechariah 5 as well). Juxtapose Deuteronomy with Revelation's similar language as Jesus opens the seals, bowls, trumpets, and woes. It is Jesus Christ Who opens Revelation's seals! Likewise, He dictates the trumpets, woes, hail, fire, and those creepy locust things with crowns, scorpion tails, faces, hair, and lion's teeth. Jesus is both the Lion and the Lamb.

It may be difficult for us to grasp that our God brings about such destructive judgments, but He does. It is written in the same Book that also reveals His love towards mankind through the death of His Son, Jesus. Mankind brought sin into the world and this is how God will bring sin to an end. It is the closing curtain leading to a new heavens and a new earth wherein righteousness dwells. All of which is very intense.

Chew on these ardent words from Peter:

> *The Lord is not slack concerning His promise, as some count slackness, but is longsuffering toward us, not willing that any should perish but that all should come to repentance. 10 But the day of the Lord will come as a thief in the night, in which the heavens will pass away with a great noise, and the elements will melt with fervent heat; both the earth and the works that are in it will be burned up. 11 Therefore, since all these things will be dissolved, what manner of persons ought you to be in holy conduct and godliness, 12 looking for and hastening the coming of the day of God, because of which the heavens will be dissolved, being on fire, and the elements will melt with fervent heat? 13 Nevertheless we, according to His promise, look for new heavens and a new earth in which righteousness dwells.*
>
> *2 Peter 3:9-13*

Chapter 8

Behind the Veil of Idols

David and Goliath

We all love the story of David and Goliath. The hero, David, saves Israel from the Philistines with a sling and a stone — and his God. From within this story many preachers have preached, many children have dreamed, and many enemies have feared. For within this story is the depths of a man, no a boy, who loved and trusted his God. I too will draw from deep within David's exploits to this Philistine, for a final blow to this wind of doctrine so many in the church cling to:

> So the Philistine came, and began drawing near to David, and the man who bore the shield went before him. 42 And when the Philistine looked about and saw David, he disdained him; for he was only a youth, ruddy and good-looking. 43 So the Philistine said to David, "Am I a dog, that you come to me with sticks?" And the Philistine cursed <07043> David by his gods. 44 And the Philistine said to David, "Come to me, and I will give your flesh to the birds of the air and the beasts of the field!" 45 Then David said to the Philistine, "You come to me with a sword, with a spear, and with a javelin. But I come to you in the name of the LORD of hosts, the God of the armies of Israel, whom you have defied. 46 This day the LORD will deliver you into my hand, and I will strike you and take your head from you. And this day I will give the carcasses of the camp of the Philistines to the birds of the air and the wild beasts of the earth, that all the earth may know that there is a God in Israel. 47 "Then all this assembly shall know that the LORD does not save with sword and spear; for the battle is the LORD'S, and He will give you into our hands."
>
> *1 Samuel 17:41-47*

Verse 43 says Goliath cursed David by his gods. From 1 Corinthians 10:19-22 we find demons are behind the veil of idols. Though the idol itself is nothing there are demonic spirits behind the scenes. Therefore people sacrifice to demons when they sacrifice to their idols. With this in mind, let's view what Goliath said to David. Since Goliath cursed David by his gods, if ever there was an example of spirit activity riding on a curse it would be here. But what was David's response? Profoundly, "You, Goliath, come at me with what you have and I'll come to you with Who I have!" David knew the curse meant nothing with God on his side. David knew God was enough!

Do we?

Watermarks

Every page in the New Testament must be read with certain backdrops. These backdrops watermark everything Jesus said and did. Among these backdrops is the fact that Jesus only did what He saw the Father doing and only said what He heard the Father saying. As we form our theology and doctrine, we must keep that fact in mind. When Jesus spoke to the storm, it was because He either saw or heard the Father. Likewise, when Jesus spoke in Matthew 23 to the scribes and Pharisees He was not binding them with His words, He was pointing out facts the Father revealed.

Under the New Covenant, being partakers of the Holy Spirit, we have become a new creation. Through this Covenant we have been given many promises, all of which are apprehended through faith by means of the Holy Spirit's indwelling. His indwelling, though secure, must be yielded to. This life is Christ in us: a life of yielding to what He is doing and what He is saying. He did not transfer power to us making us some sort of a god-man, He is that power. Independent of us, and yet one with us in spirit.

He is God, we are not.

Section 2

Generational Curses

The Author

I understand more than the ancients,
Because I keep Your precepts.
Psalm 119:99

WHAT WE BELIEVE is our filter for everything. Our beliefs dictate our worldview and how we walk before God. They determine how we see people, sin, disease, and life. What we believe matters. What we believe about the Bible matters even more. What the Bible actually says matters most.

A newlywed couple came for help. Because they were unable to communicate feely, specifically the husband to the wife, they believed generational curses generated through demonic attachments were the roots. Curses, somehow... somewhere... in his family line, must be the reason and they must be broken. They believed anointing their house to break these curses was the only solution. After a brief dialog it became apparent there was nothing abnormal. It was normal newlywed life. I encouraged them to relax and just get to know one another better. In time all would work itself out. If they had continued believing their problems were inescapable due to a curse, their actions would have followed synchronized with their beliefs. In the end nothing would have changed. Anointing oil on the door posts or breaking family curses would have changed nothing, since there wasn't a curse to break. Last I heard, twenty years later, they are still happily married.

Once my husband found a college student curled up in a little ball sobbing desperately. It turns out she'd been through a "deliverance" session a few weeks previous. In this session she had "received deliverance" from demons and generational curses. But now she found herself dealing with the same issues she had been "delivered" from. Why? First, her problems weren't generational curses, they were sin. And secondly, having probably gotten some relief from demons, she hadn't been taught about how demons behave—though they leave, they often come back. (Even when our doctrine is wrong the Name of Jesus still dispels demons.) She needed teaching on how to stand her ground in Jesus and war a good warfare. Satan, remember, left Jesus until there was a better opportunity (Luke 4:13). Demons look for opportunities.

Both of the above stories show how our beliefs dictate our approach to life and its struggles. If our paradigm is that generational curses control our life, then our approach to our life's problems will be, at best, an allusive pathway. We will be aiming at a target that doesn't exist, never able to overcome. However, if we approach life's problems within the confines of NT teaching, then we will find the freedom and victory we long for.

Chapter 9

Old Testament

GENERATIONAL CURSES ARE AN obvious part of the OT. The Law of First Mention takes us back to the Garden of Eden where the most potent of all generational curses was set in motion. The author was God. Generational curses were imputed due to sin. And therein lies the pattern of generational curses. Biblical generational curses all have these three fundamentals in common:

- God was always the author/imputer of the curse.
- Generational curses were always judgment for sin.
- Generational curses could not be broken off by another person; they could only be repented of, and then, only if God allowed it.

Some generational curses had a time limit (Exodus 20:5), while others continued (2 Samuel 12:10). Following are a few examples from the OT.

Mankind through Adam: Genesis 2-3

And the LORD God commanded the man, saying, "Of every tree of the garden you may freely eat; 17 but of the tree of the knowledge of good and evil you shall not eat, for in the day that you eat of it you shall surely die."

Genesis 2:16-17

Of all generational curses the first and most devastating occurred in Genesis 3. Because of one man all generations have been born into and under this curse. Herein lies the questions: what exactly did God say would happen if they ate from the tree?

God told the man: *"...for in the day that you eat of it you shall surely die."* Yet it took nearly 1000 years for Adam to die physically. How then did Adam die that day? Spiritually. Immediately. Once sin entered Adam and Eve died—spiritually. Instantaneously they needed redemption. God in Genesis said to Adam: *"...Till you return to the ground, For out of it you were taken; For dust you are, And to dust you shall return" (Genesis 3:19). "Till you return to the ground"* implies a length of time until Adam and Eve would die physically. Interestingly, 2 Peter 3:8 says that *with the Lord one day is as a thousand years, and a thousand years as one day.* So even physically they died in "that day." From Romans: *just as through one man [Adam] sin entered the world, and death through sin, and thus death spread to all men, because all sinned...(Romans 5:12).* Clearly death came through sin. Yet, Romans 5:17 says: *For if by the one man's offense death reigned through the one, much more those who receive abundance of grace and of the gift of righteousness will reign in life through the One, Jesus Christ.*

When someone receives Jesus they are immediately transferred from death to life—spiritually. Jesus said in John 10:10: *"I have come that they may have life, and that they may have it more abundantly."* Furthermore, 1 John 5:12 states: *He who has the Son has life; he who does not have the Son of God does not have life.* And John 5:24: *"Most assuredly, I say to you, he who hears My word and believes in Him who sent Me has everlasting life, and shall not come into judgment, but has passed from death into life."* These scriptures do not mean that all the suddenly when someone receives Jesus Christ they start breathing. Rather, they have life—spiritually. They have immediately passed from death to life and will live eternally with God. Instantaneously the generational curse from the Garden is broken. "You shall surely die" is replaced with "you shall not perish, but have eternal life." As the curse brought immediate spiritual death to all generations through Adam, Jesus imparts spiritual life, immediately breaking the curse to all who receive Him.

Concerning physical death: it took nearly 1000 years for sin to take its toll on the man and woman God had created. Sin finally killed Adam and Eve. Spiritually and physically the wages of sin is always death. Physical death was and is the natural consequence of sin in and on the human body. But physical death was not the curse; the curse was: *"for in the day that you eat of it you shall surely die."* Physical death was the consequence—spiritual death was the curse. However, God provided for our natural bodies as well. Jesus, having raised from the dead, will also raise us up together with Him:

> *Behold, I tell you a mystery: We shall not all sleep, but we shall all be changed — 52 in a moment, in the twinkling of an eye, at the last trumpet. For the trumpet will sound, and the dead will be raised incorruptible, and we shall be changed. 53 For this corruptible must put on incorruption, and this mortal must put on immortality. 54 So when this corruptible has put on incorruption, and this mortal has put on immortality, then shall be brought to pass the saying that is written: "Death is swallowed up in victory."*
>
> 1 Corinthians 15:51-54

Eve

> *To the woman He said: "I will greatly multiply your sorrow and your conception; In pain you shall bring forth children; Your desire shall be for your husband, And he shall rule over you."*
>
> Genesis 3:16

> *But women will be preserved <4982: sozo> through the bearing of children if they continue in faith and love and sanctity with self-restraint.*
>
> 1 Timothy 2:15 NASV

Though women still have pain in child birth, 1 Timothy 2:15 is in the context of the Garden and the fall of mankind. The word sozo is linked to what Jesus purchased for us and is usually translated "save." Therefore, regarding God multiplying women's pain in childbirth, though it is not referred to as a curse, and though pain still remains, Jesus' sozo reaches even into childbearing.

Second Commandment

> *"You shall not make for yourself a carved image, or any likeness of anything that is in heaven above, or that is in the earth beneath, or that is in the water under the earth; 5 you shall not bow down to them nor serve them. For I, the LORD your God, am a jealous God, visiting the iniquity of the fathers on the children to the third and fourth*

generations of those who hate Me, 6 but showing mercy to thousands, to those who
love Me and keep My commandments.

Exodus 20:4-6

Interestingly, I often hear verse 5 partially quoted by those who want to
promote their theology of generational curses. They say something like,
"to the third or fourth generation," as they ascribe curses to the devil. But
I have never, in over 20 years, heard anyone quote verse 5 accurately,
completely, or continue with its context into verse 6 (*but showing mercy to*
thousands, to those who love Me and keep My commandments). Furthermore,
no one has ever quoted verse 5 to me accurately noting the proper author
as God: *For I, the* LORD *your God, am a jealous God, visiting the iniquity of the*
fathers on the children to the third and fourth generations of those who hate Me.
Who is visiting the iniquity of the fathers to the children? It is none other
than the LORD our God.

Eli

The LORD said to Samuel, "Behold, I am about to do a thing in Israel at which both
ears of everyone who hears it will tingle. 12 In that day I will carry out against Eli all
that I have spoken concerning his house, from beginning to end. 13 For I have told
him that I am about to judge his house forever for the iniquity which he knew, because
his sons brought a curse <07043> on themselves and he did not rebuke them. 14
Therefore I have sworn to the house of Eli that the iniquity of Eli's house shall not be
atoned for by sacrifice or offering forever."

1 Samuel 3:11-14 NASV

1 Samuel 4 describes the events just as God has said: …*the ark of God was*
taken; and the two sons of Eli, Hophni and Phinehas, died (1 Samuel 4:11). And
when Eli heard the news he fell over backwards and died. God judged
the house of Eli. He would not allow atonement for their iniquity (1
Samuel 3:14). This curse was not allowed to be broken by repentance.

David

[God through Nathan the prophet to David] …'Why have you despised the
commandment of the LORD, to do evil in His sight? You have killed Uriah the Hittite
with the sword; you have taken his wife to be your wife, and have killed him with the
sword of the people of Ammon. 10 'Now therefore, the sword shall never depart from

your house, because you have despised Me, and have taken the wife of Uriah the Hittite to be your wife.' 11 "Thus says the LORD: 'Behold, I will raise up adversity against you from your own house; and I will take your wives before your eyes and give them to your neighbor, and he shall lie with your wives in the sight of this sun. 12 'For you did it secretly, but I will do this thing before all Israel, before the sun.'" 13 So David said to Nathan, "I have sinned against the LORD." And Nathan said to David, "The LORD also has put away your sin; you shall not die. 14 However, because by this deed you have given great occasion to the enemies of the LORD to blaspheme, the child also who is born to you shall surely die."

2 Samuel 12:9-14

God said: *"…I will raise up adversity against you from your own house; and I will take your wives before your eyes and give them to your neighbor, and he shall lie with your wives in the sight of this sun (2 Samuel 12:11)."* Everything Nathan prophesied came to pass exactly as God had said it would: the child died, Absalom took the throne (2 Samuel 15) and *raped David's concubines in the sight of all Israel* (2 Samuel 16:22), and the sword didn't depart from David's house (2 Samuel 13:32). No remedy was allowed.

The Kings of Judah from Ahaz to Josiah

From Ahaz to Josiah there were five kings. Ahaz was wicked, but he was the father of Hezekiah who was righteous. God said of Hezekiah that there was no other king like him, either before or after him (2 Kings 18). But his son Manasseh was so wicked that God said Manasseh's sin was the reason He led Judah into captivity (Jeremiah 15:4). Manasseh, who repented in his later years, had a son named Amon who also was wicked. Amon had a son named Josiah who was a strong righteous reformer. If generational curses were passed apart from God's sovereign will, then generational curses would be passed from Ahaz to Hezekiah and from Amon to Josiah. But they were not. God authors and imputes generational curses—every one of them.

We must conclude generational curses were part of the OT. And yet, God created each individual with a free choice to either choose life or death, obedience or rebellion, wickedness or righteousness, faith or unbelief. Generational curses were not a finite determination as to whether or not someone would serve God. A heart for God has always been matter of personal choice, as we can see from the examples of the kings above. One king was righteous and his son was not, and another king was wicked and his son was the most loyal to God there ever was in Judah (2 Kings 18:5). We were created with a free will. After all, Adam sinned for all of us, but who was his father passing down generational curses to him? And though a generational curse was on David's linage, not all his children were wicked or killers. Messiah Jesus came through David's linage.

God is the author of generational curses. There isn't even one alternative example providing another explanation. Never the devil—not even one time. Never another person—not even one time. People cursed, but their curses had no effect. Also, there is not one example where a curse was broken off a person by another person. Only God can break a curse.

Some believe that Job, the Gibeonites (2 Samuel 21), Laban, Jacob and Rebekah are examples of generational curses. They are not. A curse was ALWAYS imputed by God and was ALWAYS judgment for sin. Family traits are not generational curses. More on family traits in Chapter 11 page 110.

Gibeonites: 2 Samuel 21

Looking at the Gibeonites in 2 Samuel 21, this is what the scriptures say: *Now there was a famine in the days of David for three years, year after year; and David inquired of the LORD. And the LORD answered, "It is because of Saul and his bloodthirsty house, because he killed the Gibeonites." (2 Samuel 21:1).* These are the facts:

1. Israel had made a covenant with the Gibeonites, not to kill them, in Joshua 9:15.
2. Saul, zealous for Israel, killed some Gibeonites, even though they were in covenant with Israel.
3. Now Saul was dead and David was king.
4. God created the famine.
5. It was because Saul killed the Gibeonites.

A generational curse is in the family line. This was a famine—in creation—the weather patterns. God created a famine, so David would inquire, God would answer, and things would be made right regarding Saul's slaughter of the Gibeonites. This was not a generational curse.

Laban, Rebekah, and Jacob

Laban, Rebekah, and Jacob's deceptive ways are learned behavior—a family trait passed down by tradition. We can also see family traits in the way that both Abraham and Isaac treated their wives. Both of them, out of fear, passed off their wife as their sister. If we look at our own lives and families, we too will see traits that have been passed from our relatives, both good and bad. But these are not God imputed generational curses due to judgment on sin. They are learned behavior.

Job

Now for Job. Job's attacks were to be endured. They could not be broken off. God was ultimately in control. The devil was only allowed so much access to Job. Job did not have a curse—he had a supervised satanic attack. In the NT, Jesus gives us power that was not available in the OT: power to trample upon serpents, scorpions, and all the power of the evil one (Luke 10:19). However, God at times allows a devil to work us over for some greater purpose; ultimately, the devil is only a tool in the hand of God. A good example of this is Paul's thorn in the flesh (2 Corinthians 12:7).

As we move on from the OT into the New, we will cross the bridge of Jeremiah 31:29-34. As Jeremiah stands in the OT viewing into the New, he hears the Holy thundering the New Covenant from deep within the chambers of Heaven: *"Behold the days are coming,"* declares the LORD...

Jeremiah's Prophecy

> *"In those days they shall say no more: 'The fathers have eaten sour grapes, And the children's teeth are set on edge.' 30 But every one shall die for his own iniquity; every man who eats the sour grapes, his teeth shall be set on edge. 31 Behold, the days are coming, says the LORD, when I will make a new covenant with the house of Israel and with the house of Judah — 32 not according to the covenant that I made with their fathers in the day that I took them by the hand to lead them out of the land of Egypt,*

My covenant which they broke, though I was a husband to them, says the LORD. 33
But this is the covenant that I will make with the house of Israel after those days, says
the LORD: I will put My law in their minds, and write it on their hearts; and I will be
their God, and they shall be My people. 34 No more shall every man teach his
neighbor, and every man his brother, saying, 'Know the LORD,' for they all shall
know Me, from the least of them to the greatest of them, says the LORD. For I will
forgive their iniquity, and their sin I will remember no more."

Jeremiah 31:29-34

Like a surveyor's pin, the herald of the glorious New Covenant is forever
fixed right in the midst of this OT prophet's writing. God declaring not
only the coming of the New, but also the way in which it is different from
the Old. The Old: *'The fathers have eaten sour grapes, And the children's teeth*
are set on edge' (31:29). The New says: *"But every one shall die for his own*
iniquity; every man who eats the sour grapes, his teeth shall be set on edge"
(31:30). In the Old, the children suffered because of the father's iniquity;
the New is personal responsibility before God. We hear personal
responsibility reverberated throughout the NT. The New Covenant,
Jeremiah prophesies about, is the same covenant where God said He
would: *"...put My law in their minds, and write it on their hearts; and I will be*
their God, and they shall be My people." The New Covenant has made the
Old obsolete (Hebrews 8:13) — generational curses included.

Chapter 10

New Covenant

Personal responsibility before god is the focus of the NT. Generational curses are buried with the Old Covenant for the people of God. Again, in the OT, curses were always pronounced by God and were always judgment for sin. The answer to our sin problem begins with Jesus; it continues with the working of the most beloved Holy Spirit within us. Our job is to apprehend by faith what Jesus provided for us. The NT has very little to say about generational curses. Therefore, this section will be short.

Blind from Birth

Now as Jesus passed by, He saw a man who was blind from birth. 2 And His disciples asked Him, saying, "Rabbi, who sinned, this man or his parents, that he was born blind?" 3 Jesus answered, "Neither this man nor his parents sinned, but that the works of God should be revealed in him. 4 I must work the works of Him who sent Me while it is day; the night is coming when no one can work. 5 As long as I am in the world, I am the light of the world." 6 When He had said these things, He spat on the ground and made clay with the saliva; and He anointed the eyes of the blind man with the clay. 7 And He said to him, "Go, wash in the pool of Siloam" (which is translated, Sent). So he went and washed, and came back seeing.

John 9:1-7

The disciples' reasoning paradigm was bent towards generational curses. They thought a generational curse was the likely cause of this man's blindness, but they were wrong. Jesus' response was basically, "No, this is not due to the sins of a father being passed down to their children. Rather, this is an opportunity for My Father's glory."

Tradition

...knowing that you were not redeemed with corruptible things, like silver or gold, from your aimless conduct received by tradition from your fathers, 19 but with the precious blood of Christ, as of a lamb without blemish and without spot. 20 He indeed was foreordained before the foundation of the world, but was manifest in these last times for you 21 who through Him believe in God, who raised Him from the dead and gave Him glory, so that your faith and hope are in God. 22 Since you have purified your souls in obeying the truth through the Spirit in sincere love of the brethren, love one another fervently with a pure heart, 23 having been born again, not of corruptible seed but incorruptible, through the word of God which lives and abides forever.

1 Peter 1:18b-23

In this epistle, Peter spotlights: *your aimless conduct received by tradition from your fathers.* The Greek word translating the phrase *"tradition from your fathers"* means (GL), "handed down from one's fathers or ancestors." Strong's defines it as, "traditionary: —received by tradition from fathers." If verse 18 stood alone, our *aimless conduct* could be thought as genetically or culturally handed down, and except for verse 22, could have included generational curses. (Recall that generational curses can only be broken by God.) Yet, verse 22 says that believers: *have purified [their] souls in obeying the truth through the Spirit.* If a generational curse was involved, "obeying the truth" would be out of the question regarding "purify our souls," for the soul could not be purified apart from God breaking the curse. This truth is echoed throughout the NT: we who are in Christ are indwelt by the Holy Spirit, we therefore, have Him and He is all we need.

1 Peter 1:14's wording: *"not conforming yourselves to the former lusts, as in your ignorance"* signifies ignorance and not imputed through a curse. It is also a command, which means we can obey it by the Holy Spirit's empowerment. We must conclude, since the Holy Spirit lives in us, we have all we need to obey God. Furthermore, the phrase: *"Be holy, for I am holy"* (1 Peter 1:16) reveals that God sees our identity as identifying with Him. He is holy and His indwelling makes us holy. Now, since we are

holy, we are to be holy. He expects our character to line up with His character.

Blessed with Believing Abraham

Therefore know that only those who are of faith are sons of Abraham. 8 And the Scripture, foreseeing that God would justify the Gentiles by faith, preached the gospel to Abraham beforehand, saying, "In you all the nations shall be blessed." 9 So then those who are of faith are blessed with believing Abraham. 10 For as many as are of the works of the law are under the curse; for it is written, "Cursed is everyone who does not continue in all things which are written in the book of the law, to do them." 11 But that no one is justified by the law in the sight of God is evident, for "the just shall live by faith." 12 Yet the law is not of faith, but "the man who does them shall live by them." 13 Christ has redeemed us from the curse of the law, having become a curse for us (for it is written, "Cursed is everyone who hangs on a tree"), 14 that the blessing of Abraham might come upon the Gentiles in Christ Jesus, that we might receive the promise of the Spirit through faith.

Galatians 3:7-14

Let's look at Galatians 3:7-14 outlined form for clarity:

- Only those of faith are sons of Abraham.
- In Abraham all the nations will be blessed.
- Those of faith are blessed with believing Abraham.
- Those relying on the law are under a curse.
- No one is justified by the law before God.
- The righteous man shall live by faith.
- The just shall live by faith.
- The law is not of faith.
- Christ has redeemed us from the curse of the law.
- Jesus became a curse for us.
- The blessing of Abraham comes upon the Gentiles in Christ Jesus.
- We receive the promise of the Spirit through faith.

In Galatians 3 we find the clearest scriptures in the NT explaining curses in sight of what Jesus Christ has done for us. We are a blessed people if we are in Jesus Christ. God nailed His judgment to the cross.

Jesus' "It is finished" thundered throughout eternity.

For a review on unbelievers and curses, *(as many as are of the works of the Law are under a curse)* refer to: Chapter 7 Last Considerations: Curses and the Unbeliever, page 90.

Summary

Generational curses are spiritually imputed. They are spiritual edicts instigated by God and manifested in the natural world. Natural genetic traits are not curses. Genetic traits are natural occurrences passed down physically. Nothing in the NT substantiates that believers can have generational curses. Life in Jesus breaks us free from our past no matter what it was: *Therefore, if anyone is in Christ, he is a new creation; old things have passed away; behold, all things have become new. 18 Now all things are of God... (2 Corinthians 5:17-18a).* We deal with consequences and habits from our sin nature, an un-renewed mind, and reaping the decisions of our pagan pilgrimage, but we have now received a generational blessing from our Father. We are in Christ! We are forgiven! We are blessed!

The end of curses...

Or is it?

There is still more to say on curses as we will see in Section 3, page 113.

Chapter 11

Family Traits

Curses with spiritual power were always enacted by God. And they were always judgment for sin. Jesus Christ, for the Christian, became a curse for us. Jesus bore our judgment for sin by dying on the cross and has completely and forever settled our guilt before God. God no longer judges us on the basis of sin. Yes, He disciplines us for our good, but judgment has forever been settled. God said He would make a new covenant that would make the old obsolete (Jeremiah 31 and Hebrews 8:13). The NT paradigm is personal responsibility before God. In view of this truth, why do we see family sins that follow family linage?

Having been to many conferences over the years, understandably some leave a greater imprint on my memory than others; some because the Holy Spirit magnified the Son and manifested His glory, while others due to less glorious imprints. Here is one of the lesser:

"A red river—a river of blood," said the prophet, "I was lifted up above a map of the United States and I saw a river of blood that I understood was my family linage. Then as I watched I saw different places along this river where generational curses occurred in my bloodlines." He then proceeded to explain how he broke off all incurred generational curses from each place where the curses had been imputed. State by state and city by city, as the bloodline flowed throughout the United States, he rendered the curses powerless. He is an international well-known prophet. I was astonished as I listened and watched as the audience ate up the meal he fed them. How could this man possibly be speaking for

God? Not a chance! All revelations must line up with biblical doctrine, and this one clearly did not. The winds were blowing!

What we believe determines what we think about God and His ways. It determines how we process information, even the information we hear from God and His word. If this prophet legitimately saw a red river by the Spirit of God, most definitely he interpreted it inaccurately. But his belief about generational curses shaped his ideology and interpretation. He therefore taught others falsely. How many went away from the conference believing they too must break curses off their linage?

In view of what we know about curses, generational or otherwise, how can we explain the evil that seems to generationally follow family lines? What is the truth about how the enemy works within families? Demons use the same tactics year after year, generation after generation, century after century. They just aren't that creative. But if we are ignorant of Satan's devices, he may outwit us. Following are a couple hypothetical examples of the ways I see that the enemy works through generations.

Example 1: A father abused his child. He was abused by his father and as far back as anyone knows, this has been the history of the family, generation after generation. It could just as well be alcoholism, legalism, or racism. The way the enemy works is the same. So how does the enemy work? Demons know how people were raised; they know how their fathers were raised; they know there is a family weakness in one generation, because of the culture of a previous generation. And this weakness will likely be the enemy's first area of attack, and second, and third. This family's culture is already bent towards abuse more than a family where abuse was never a part of its culture. When the enemy attacks in this area, a conditioning for this temptation already exists. Because of this conditioning there is a greater chance of success for the enemy's temptation to conceive and become an act. However, someone who was raised in a family where abuse never occurred, a thought of abuse immediately would be rejected. It would never be allowed to take root.

Example 2: Consider if someone was raised in a family full of pornography. Magazines and movies were everywhere. Filthy movies were an evening occurrence. Now as a teen their mind is full of images; their body gets engaged. Soon they too will likely become a slave to pornography and immorality. Fornication becomes their way of life. Later they receive Jesus, but find they can't seem to get free from their addictions. What is happening? First, the enemy knows their weaknesses and he is determined to keep them in bondage. Pornography seems to be his best bet, since it's already in his family history. So what does the enemy do? He doubles up on the temptation, and he is not passive about it. He bombards the new Christian with thoughts and with whispers. The enemy reminds them of the images they had seen and the people they had been with sexually. He makes sure people the new Christian was immoral with are around a lot. (After all they're the devil's slaves anyway.) Now the new Christian has a choice to make. Will they fight the good fight of faith or will they cave, returning again to their life of death? If they choose freedom, it will be hard work, but it means life and peace. Their mind must be renewed; their thoughts must be taken captive. This is not a curse that can be broken off. It is a life that must be changed; a mind that must be renewed.

These examples are not generational curses. They are learned sinful lifestyles. For the sake of clarity and accuracy and to avoid confusion we ought to use terminology as the Bible uses it. If we use the word "curse" in a way the Bible does not, we may understand what we are saying and our doctrine behind our words, but the listener may not. There is a chance they will either walk away with an obscured view of curses and how to be free or they'll be confused about the truth of the Bible.

Learned behavior usually isn't just broken off someone by prayer. Of course God can do this, but He usually chooses to help us fight to get the victory over sin. God could have wiped out all the wicked nations in the OT, but He chose rather to help Israel fight them. Jesus purchased our freedom on the cross and it belongs to us, but we need to fight to possess and walk in that freedom, and that typically takes a lot of hard work. Yet, the Holy Spirit helps us and He works in us what is pleasing to God.

Section 3

Heavens and Earth

Slavery to Corruption

Rivers of water run down from my eyes,
Because men do not keep Your law.
Psalm 119:136

Thus far we've studied curses on mankind: curses imputed by God and those spoken by people. We found God's curses are the only curses with spiritual power. People curse for sure, but their curses carry absolutely no spiritual power. God's words alone have creative power.

In this last section we will look at curses on creation. How did death enter creation and was it a result of a curse? If so, then was it reversed under the New Covenant? These questions will be addressed in this Section.

For the creation was subjected to futility, not willingly, but because of Him who subjected it, in hope that the creation itself also will be set free from its slavery to corruption into the freedom of the glory of the children of God.

Romans 8:20

Chapter 12

———·❦·⊱———

The Beginning

We CANNOT COMPREHEND THE RAMIFACATIONS of sin on the earth. Neither can we fathom how far reaching it is into creation. Imagine what it may have been like before sin entered the world and death through sin. A world devoid of death, chaos, and confusion. A world without fear; prey and predator didn't exist. Mankind was at peace with the animal kingdom. The elements were in harmony with the earth. No hurricanes. No tornados. No racial tensions. No terrorism. No wars. No bombs. The lion laid down with the lamb.

All death, in its various forms, is the result of sin — that one sin committed in the Garden: *Therefore, just as through one man sin entered the world, and death through sin, and thus death spread to all men, because all sinned (Romans 5:12).* Death also spread on account of that one sin throughout all creation. Consequently, due to one sin, creation itself is in slavery to corruption. (Romans 8:20) This fact dictates that death did not exist until man was created and then sinned.

In this Chapter we will lay a foundation in Genesis 3 by looking at the Law of First Mention. After establishing Genesis 3 as the foundation, we will then flow through the scriptures all the way to Revelation. What is the testimony of scripture regarding curses on creation beginning to end?

The Genesis: In the Beginning

"Cursed is the ground because of you," thundered God, as His resounding curse vectored through time. Thus, the first curse in recorded in history:

> Then to Adam He said, *"Because you have listened to the voice of your wife, and have eaten from the tree about which I commanded you, saying, 'You shall not eat from it'; Cursed <0779> is the ground because of you; In toil you will eat of it All the days of your life. 18 Both thorns and thistles it shall grow for you; And you will eat the plants of the field; 19 By the sweat of your face You will eat bread, Till you return to the ground, Because from it you were taken; For you are dust, And to dust you shall return."*
>
> *Genesis 3:17-19 NASB*

The earth, now staggering under the gravity of God's curse, changed radically. How Adam and Eve must have mourned as the ground exchanged its plenty for thorns and thistles. Death had been foreign to them, but now it was woven into every plant, every animal, and every child they bore. Even in their very own flesh, death began to reign. Did they ever wonder what God meant when He said they would return to the ground and to dust? How devastating their choice to eat the fruit that day.

Presently, we are so accustomed to death's reign in creation that without the Holt Spirit's help we don't recognize its comprehensive influence. Everything has changed! Sin ushered upheaval into all creation. Devastating as this is, the world that now exists, is not outside the sovereign control of God. Even death itself bows to His presence. God uses creation's confusion for purposes far greater than we can imagine. Consider that through the Flood He used death itself to purge sin from the earth. Looking ahead, He will again purge sin from the earth, howbeit, next time by fire (2 Peter 3:9-13).

As I consider the gravity of sin woven into the very fabric of creation, I too am met with the incredible kindness of God. Currently, we are in the midst 2018 Olympics. Snow is unnatural on the earth in a world where sin does not exist, and yet, we find we adapt to it very well. We even enjoy it, though we cannot survive its extremes. Genesis describes the immediate changes in the earth's vegetation after God cursed the ground; it would now take hard work to cultivate. The chaotic upheaval during the time of the Flood as described in Psalms 104, states the mountains rose and the valleys lowered. Such change in the landscape would cause extreme temperature variation upon the land. Since it hadn't rained previously (Genesis 2:5-6), rain itself would have been unnatural. During the Flood, the whole atmosphere changed. Genesis 2:6 says instead of rain a *mist used to rise from the earth and water the whole surface of the ground.* Now, post-Flood, the ramifications for land without rain are devastating. God even describes His withholding rain as a curse on the land. About 100 years after the Flood Peleg was born. During Peleg's days the earth was divided (Genesis 10:25). Likely, the earth had one land mass until Peleg (Genesis 1:9) and it was during his life the continents began to separate.

God: the Weather Man

Above are some of the results of sin's wages upon and in creation. Although chaos ensured, wreaking havoc on the earth and its people, God, in the midst of this chaos, has made the earth habitable for His creation. Howbeit, not all of it. God even intervenes and uses this chaos in creation for His purposes and glory. Following are a few examples:

Noah and the Flood: Genesis 6

As we read through the flood, we easily see in it God's sovereign role. He allowed the people to rule within their own hearts and they chose to remain wicked. God, however, ruled the weather and thus, the flood. The people, nevertheless, remained wicked and they paid the price for their rebellion to God. He purged the earth and cleansed it by means of the Flood for the earth was filled with violence through them (Genesis 6).

Moses: Exodus 9:23-25

Exodus' first few chapters tell of God delivering His people from Pharaoh's clutches in Egypt. God's control over His creation was on full display. Not only did God display His sovereignty over the weather in Egypt, but also over all creation, save the hearts of mankind; even darkness and death bow to His command.

Joshua and the Amorites: Joshua 10:10-14

Joshua went to war knowing God had given the Amorites into his hands. God's personal attention and sovereignty is woven throughout these scriptures. Verse 11 states that God was hurling large hailstones on the Amorites, killing many. (Can you imagine?!) Then, the LORD, because Joshua asked Him to, made the sun and moon stand still for about 24 hours (10:12).

Solomon: 2 Chronicles 7

In 2 Chronicles 7, God echoes the blessings and curses He stated back in Deuteronomy. Deuteronomy's blessings and curses are diametrically associated with God controlling the weather on behalf of His peoples' righteousness or disobedience. God said to Solomon in a dream:

> *"I have heard your prayer, and have chosen this place for Myself as a house of sacrifice. 13 When I shut up heaven and there is no rain, or command the locusts to devour the land, or send pestilence among My people, 14 if My people who are called by My name will humble themselves, and pray and seek My face, and turn from their wicked ways, then I will hear from heaven, and will forgive their sin and heal their land.*
>
> 2 Chronicles 7:12-14

Haggai to Zerubbabel: Haggai 1

During the time of Haggai's prophecy, God's people were distracted. They were supposed to be building God's house. They were, however, instead consumed with building their own homes. Here is God's response to them:

> *"Therefore the heavens above you withhold the dew, and the earth withholds its fruit. 11 For I [God] called for a drought on the land and the mountains, on the grain and*

the new wine and the oil, on whatever the ground brings forth, on men and livestock, and on all the labor of your hands."

Haggai 1:10-11

God directly took credit for the weather pattern. He called for a drought and the earth stopped producing. The people of God, in this case, had the proper response: they believed and obeyed the words of God through the prophet Haggai and began to rebuild.

The scriptures above, and others like them, reveal it is God who controls weather patterns and not us. As we look through the OT, and into the NT, we easily see God's intervention via weather. Weather, when directly related to the sin or righteousness of God's people, we can understand to be the blessings or curses God described in Deuteronomy. In the NT, Jesus commanded a storm and it dissipated. However Paul's ship in Acts 27 was wrecked in a severe storm. Consider that if weather was at Paul's command, then would he not have commanded it to cease and desist? Until the time of new heavens and the new earth, wherein dwells righteousness, we will deal with creation's chaos. Yes, we pray, asking God to avert disasters, but still, sometimes, disasters come.

Chapter 13

Grasping God's Judgments

As we approach the end of our study, we must ponder the reality of God's judgments on the depravity of mankind. This will set a paradigm for the judgments to come. Yes, God is love and yes, God kills the wicked. When He does so, it isn't to pacify some unearthed anger imbedded in His Person so that in a raging swipe of His sword He smites the ungodly. No, rather, it is to establish righteousness. As we peruse through the pages of the OT we read of peoples who were utterly and desperately wicked. Peoples who would not repent and turn to God. Peoples who filled the land with their abominations. Peoples whose descendants after them, if the linage was allowed to continue, would do the same, spreading their wickedness throughout the earth. Persistent wickedness invites God intervention.

Introducing God's Nature

In the beginning God created the heavens and the earth. 2 The earth was without form, and void; and darkness was on the face of the deep. And the Spirit of God was hovering over the face of the waters.

3 Then God said, "Let there be light"; and there was light. 4 And God saw the light, that it was good; and God divided the light from the darkness.

Genesis 1:1-4

In these scriptures, where there was chaos, confusion, and darkness, God brought order and light. He then separated the light from the darkness. It is an outflow of His nature to bring light where there is darkness and order where there is chaos. As God intervenes in the physical realm, He also intervenes in the spiritual realm, bringing light where there is darkness and order where there is chaos. Though sometimes God will bring about chaos to ultimately bring order, as we see in the Apocalypse and Babel. Gazing through the corridors of time, we see God's fingerprints ushering in the new heavens and the new earth. He has and will again purge the earth of wickedness to establish righteousness.

Cleansing the Earth

To set the stage for what God will do at the end of this age, we will first look briefly at times when God destroyed peoples due to their utter wickedness. God dealt with the wickedness of specific cities, nations, and people. Three times we see a worldwide cleansing: first, during the Flood; second, in part at the end of this age; followed by a complete cleansing at the end of the Millennial Age. As we work through the following scriptures, keep in mind all events are watermarked with the God who loved so much that He died for us and for all humanity. This is the same God who cleanses the earth of wickedness for the sake of righteousness.

The Flood: Genesis 6-9

> *Then the LORD saw that the wickedness of man was great in the earth, and that every intent of the thoughts of his heart was only evil continually.*
>
> *6 And the LORD was sorry that He had made man on the earth, and He was grieved in His heart. 7 So the LORD said, "I will destroy man whom I have created from the face of the earth, both man and beast, creeping thing and birds of the air, for I am sorry that I have made them."*
>
> Genesis 6:5-7

This is the first time God purged the earth due to the conduct and character of people. (People's righteousness or sin determine God's dealings with the earth.) All living things having the breath of life were destroyed, except what was safe on the Ark (Genesis 7:21-23).

Babel: Genesis 11:1-9

Babel means confusion. Though God didn't destroy the people of Babel, He did intervene to stop their plans. Babel is prophetic in nature, being the headwaters of Babylon. Babylon, the Harlot, is the mysterious wicked city in Revelation. Here in Genesis 11, the people sought to build themselves a city made out of slim and clay (11:3), in contrast to Abraham who sought the city whose builder and maker was God — New Jerusalem (Hebrews 11:10) made of precious stones and pure gold (Revelation 21:18-19). Babel, built in a plain, was likely more a spiritual endeavor than a natural. Who builds a tower to reach into Heaven (:4) starting in a valley? Furthermore, the echoes of Satan's "I wills" from Isaiah 14:13-14 are easily heard in Babel's valley. Some liken Nimrod, the architect of Babel, to the antichrist, the Assyrian.

Sodom and Gomorrah: Genesis 13-19

God utterly destroyed Sodom and Gomorrah (19:24-25), because: *the men of Sodom were exceedingly wicked and sinful against the LORD* (13:13). Even with God in their midst, the Sodomites stiffened their necks against Him and would not repent. In their depravity, these men pressed against Lot's house so that they could get to the angels[1] to rape them (Genesis 19:1-13). Peter 2 compares Sodom and Gomorrah to the ungodly at the end of this age, exemplifying their destruction and judgement to come.

Canaan: Deuteronomy 7:1-2

Canaan was terribly wicked. Israel was told to cross the Jordan and utterly destroy the peoples that occupied the land therein. However, God said this not because of Israel's righteousness, rather it was due to the wickedness of the Canaanites that they were to be destroyed (Deuteronomy 9:1-5). Ezra 9 says that the Canaanites had made the land unclean having, with their abominations *filled it from one end to another with their impurity*. We easily read through these stories and miss the

---

[1] A theophanic angel is a manifestation of God as an angel that is tangible to the human senses in the OT. In Genesis 18 and 19 we find God, the Trinity, represented as angels, men, and as the LORD.

Canaanites' utter depravity. Their high places were alters of sacrifice where they burned their children to demon gods, passing them through the fire.

Many times we read of God assisting the Israelites in their military endeavors as they utterly wiped out the inhabitants of the land. Other times it was God who acted alone, as the Israelites marched or sang or beat drums or blew trumpets. Their conquests are illustrations to us typifying the cleansing of the land, the destruction of the wicked, and the ushering in of righteousness at the end of the age.

Chapter 14

An End for a New Beginning

Were order, harmony, and righteousness brought back into creation through the Cross or is creation still staggering from the weight of mankind's sin and the curse imposed by God? Consider that the covenant God made through the blood of Christ is with mankind and not creation. Those who enter into covenant with God through Jesus, have eternal life. Though their bodies will die, they will be raised to live with God forever. In this age, even when God intervenes, death, infused into creation in the Garden, in the end, reigns. Lazarus died again. Howbeit, those given new bodies when Christ returns will die no more. Creation receives redemption after the return of Christ and the 1000 year Millennial Age.

The following study of Romans 8, 2 peter 3, and Revelation 21-22 will wrap up our discussion on curses. These three sections of scripture reveal the end of God's curse on creation, His purpose in ending creation's curse, and when it will end.

Looking Forward: Romans 8

For the earnest expectation of the creation eagerly waits for the revealing of the sons of God. 20 For the creation was subjected to futility[1], not willingly, but because of Him who subjected it in hope; 21 because the creation itself also will be delivered from

---

[1] Futility: 3153 ματαιότης mataiotes mat-ah-yot'-ace
1) what is devoid of truth and appropriateness 2) perverseness, depravity 3) frailty, want of vigour

the bondage of corruption into the glorious liberty of the children of God. 22 For we know that the whole creation groans and labors with birth pangs together until now. 23 Not only that, but we also who have the firstfruits of the Spirit, even we ourselves groan within ourselves, eagerly waiting for the adoption, the redemption of our body.

Romans 8:19-23

Verse 19 states that creation itself is anxiously awaiting the revealing of the sons of God. Why? Because God subjected creation to futility (20), when He cursed creation, way back in Genesis 3. But God subjected it in hope, looking forward to creation being set free from its slavery to corruption (20-22). When will creation's freedom from its curse come? It is at the end of the Millennial Age; at the time of the judgment of the ungodly; at the time of the New Heavens and the New Earth. As we live in hope looking forward to our full redemption, creation too is awaiting its freedom from death and corruption.

Beginning of the End: 2 Peter 3

But the day of the Lord will come as a thief in the night, in which the heavens will pass away with a great noise, and the elements will melt with fervent heat; both the earth and the works that are in it will be burned up.

11 Therefore, since all these things will be dissolved, what manner of persons ought you to be in holy conduct and godliness, 12 looking for and hastening the coming of the day of God, because of which the heavens will be dissolved, being on fire, and the elements will melt with fervent heat? 13 Nevertheless we, according to His promise, look for new heavens and a new earth in which righteousness dwells.

2 Peter 3:10-13

Peter's writing in 2 Peter 3 spans from Genesis all the way to the new heavens and the new earth. The heavens and the earth are described as reserved for fire and kept for the day of judgment and destruction of ungodly men, and the heavens as passing away with a roar and being destroyed by burning; the elements will be destroyed with intense heat and the earth and its works burned up. Why does God pronounce such a harsh sentence upon the heavens and earth? Why does He destroy His creation? For the sake of righteousness. Righteousness is His heart, His purpose—His resolute determination. So profound His desire for righteousness that He sent His Son to die for us so that we could become His righteous (2 Corinthians 5:21). God promised a new heavens and earth wherein righteousness dwells. He does away with the present heavens and earth, and destroys the wicked who will not repent for the sake of righteousness.

The Appointed Time: 2 Thessalonians 2 and Daniel 8

Both Paul and Daniel describe the end-time reign of the antichrist: *the lawless one is according to the working[1] of Satan.* At the appointed time in human history when human wickedness reaches its full potential, the devil will have a man ready and waiting at the helm. When this lawless one—this king—arises: *the transgressors [will have] have reached their fullness (NIV: when rebels have become completely wicked) (Daniel 8:23).* Inspired and empowered by Satan, this lawless one: *through his cunning he shall cause deceit to prosper under his rule (Daniel 8:25).* His working is: *according to the working of Satan, with all power, signs, and lying wonders, 10 and with all unrighteous deception among those who perish, because they did not receive the love of the truth, that they might be saved (2 Thessalonians 2:9-10).* Concurrent with this evil one's activity: *God will send them strong delusion, that they should believe the lie, 12 that they all may be condemned who did not believe the truth but had pleasure in unrighteousness (2 Thessalonians 2:11-12).* Both God and Satan are ripening these end-time people to their utmost potential of wickedness, though they are vastly opposed in their motivations to do so. Satan rabidly hungers for whatever belongs to God (see Isaiah 14). He, in his hatred for God and mankind, endeavors furiously to set up his own kingdom to thwart the establishment of the New Jerusalem, where his arch enemy, Jesus, will reign as King of Kings. God, on the other hand, in preparation for the new heavens and the new earth, sends these end-time insurrectionists a deluding influence, in order that the fullness of their wickedness would mature and God would judge them. God does not change their nature, rather He magnifies what is already in them. This is very severe, but their utter depravity endorses God's righteousness judgments.

---

[1] 1753 ἐνέργεια energeia en-erg'-i-ah
1) working, efficiency
1a) in the NT used only of superhuman power, whether of God or of the Devil

The End is the New Beginning: Revelation 21-22

Now I saw a new heaven and a new earth, for the first heaven and the first earth had passed away. Also there was no more sea. 2 Then I, John, saw the holy city, New Jerusalem, coming down out of heaven from God, prepared as a bride adorned for her husband. 3 And I heard a loud voice from heaven saying, "Behold, the tabernacle of God is with men, and He will dwell with them, and they shall be His people. God Himself will be with them and be their God. 4 And God will wipe away every tear from their eyes; there shall be no more death, nor sorrow, nor crying. There shall be no more pain, for the former things have passed away." 5 Then He who sat on the throne said, "Behold, I make all things new." And He said to me, "Write, for these words are true and faithful."

Revelation 21:1-5

And there shall be no more curse <2652>, but the throne of God and of the Lamb shall be in it, and His servants shall serve Him.

Revelation 22:3

This end of all curses is subsequent to the storyline leading up to Revelation 22. The tribulation (Mark 13, Matthew 24), the rise of the beast (Revelation 17), apostasy (2 Thessalonians 2:3, 1 Timothy 4:1), the fall of Babylon (Revelation 18), the Return of Jesus Christ and the first resurrection (1 Thessalonians 4:17), the Millennial Age (Revelation 20), and the maturing of the Bride (Revelation 19) all precede the final blow to curses.

Revelation 21:4 describes the end of death and 22:3 the end of any curse. Interestingly, Revelation 22:3 is the only place this word translated "curse <2652>" is used; it stands as a gravestone within its context. (The NASV adds "any" before curse, and the Amplified and NSV both add the word "anything," hence nothing cursed will be in the City.) John sees the City—New Jerusalem descending out of heaven, her gates, and her foundations, beautifully adorned as a Bride. He sees the river flowing from the Throne, trees whose leaves bring healing to the nations, and light beaming forth from the radiance of God Himself. Then, in the midst of this scenery the Holy Spirit pens, "And there shall be no more curse," juxtaposing the intense reality of the new compared to the age where the curse reigned. Creation has been freed.

God makes all things new. His intent from the beginning is restored: godly people made in His image, living on a garden-like earth in relationship to Him, and ruling and reigning with Him...

Forever

Chapter 15

———✦•✚•✦———

Jesus

The Righteous One

Jesus, the most righteous man ever to walk on the earth did not bring civil order to governments, nor did He bring creation to its original state before death entered. Jesus said: *"My kingdom is not of this world. If My kingdom were of this world, My servants would fight, so that I should not be delivered to the Jews; but now My kingdom is not from here"* (John 18:36). Though Jesus came preaching and manifesting the Kingdom of God, He did not transform the entirety of the earth or humanity to the Kingdom of God. He made statements such as this one in Matthew: *"But if I cast out demons by the Spirit of God, surely the kingdom of God has come upon you"* (Matthew 12:28). And Jesus: *rebuked the wind and the raging of the water. And they ceased, and there was a calm (Luke 8:24),* and yet, in the future there were more storms and winds to come. Some believe righteousness within God's people spreads into creation much like water ripples from a stone's throw. They believe we can affect the elements, the land, and the order of creation through righteous living apart from direct intervention from God. However, in this one Man, Jesus Christ, we have God manifest in the flesh—the Righteous One Himself. He did not change the elements, the land, or creation except in little pockets temporarily. Those He healed died at some point. Yet, He showed what His Father and His kingdom looked like through preaching and demonstration that manifested His kingdom. Jesus said we ought to pray that His kingdom would come on earth as it is in heaven. As we pray "Your kingdom come" we are agreeing with God concerning the return of His Son and we are agreeing with Him that He will establish His kingdom on earth. There will be a time when the seventh angel sounds and: *loud voices in heaven, [will be] saying, "The kingdoms of this world have become the kingdoms of our Lord and of His Christ, and He shall reign forever and ever!" (Revelation 11:15).* What we see in part now will continue until fully established during the millennial reign of Jesus Christ. Jesus will literally sit on His throne in Jerusalem and rule the nations. We touch that millennial reign now, as we too, by the power of the Holy Spirit manifest His kingdom in this age. The scriptures bear witness of a coming kingdom age after the return of Jesus Christ, not before. In this age we partner with God as we too are led by the Holy Spirit in power, manifesting His Kingdom.

Book 2

Demons

Their Aim, Limits, and Influence

Forever, O LORD, Your word is settled in heaven.
Psalm 119:89

IN THE NEW TESTAMENT there is not a single clear scripture that states a demon can exist within a believer, whether body, soul, or spirit. There is also not a single scripture that distinctly says they cannot. Some tenets of the faith are clearly stated in the Bible, such as Jesus is the Christ, the son of the Living God. Concerning this truth the biblical evidence is overwhelmingly clear without any debating. We can go to a direct scripture stating this exact truth (John 6:69). However, whether a demon can dwell inside a believer does not have this clarity; there is not one scripture that is absolutely definitive. Therefore all doctrinal positions on whether demons can be in a Christian must be gathered from clear biblical principles using sound exegesis.

We will examine the scriptures concerning demons' aim regarding humanity and specifically Christians. We will also explore the overall emphases of the NT. Interestingly, the NT doesn't emphasize demons, which itself is insightful. Rather it focuses on Christian conduct, the church, faith, living as God's redeemed, preaching of the Gospel, salvation, authority, repentance, God's discipline, the heart of man, the power of God, God's ultimate plan, and the Kingdom of God.

As we study the work of Satan and demons, keep in mind that though their aim is to destroy humanity, God limits and restrains their activity. In the NT demons are dealt with in different ways, depending upon whether they are inside a person or not. When inside a person, they are cast out. Examples are Legion in Luke 8 and the slave girl in Acts 16. Demons outside (Jesus in Matthew 4 and Peter in Mark 8), are confronted with authority and truth. Many examples of both are in the NT. Demons influence people when and wherever possible. Our defense against their attacks is God, His word, and the authority He has given us in and through the name of Jesus.

The following are a couple of my personal experiences. I have changed the names to personify the person's theology behind their reaction.

We'll call the first person, Fearful Little-faith. Fearful was a passionate Christian and lover of God. She loved the presence of God, probably still does, and often took opportunities to pray for the sick. She'd pray for the power of God to come upon people. Once when Fearful was praying for a woman, who she'd determined was under the influence of a demon, she felt the same spirit she'd discerned in the other woman come on her. She said she plunged into despair and darkness for days. Now Fearful is no longer passionate about laying hands on people whom she doesn't know, after all they may have a demon that could get in or on her.

Next, Superstition — Superstition is also a woman who loved the things of the kingdom, at least as she knew them. She loved to prophesy, intercede, and counsel others. One Sunday we were discussing a visiting couple. The wife was visibly uncomfortable with the Charismatic flavor which our church enjoyed. On the other hand, the husband appeared he wanted to stay. He engaged in worship and conversation. Not her though. When Superstition came over to talk to me, I told her I wanted to go talk to the couple. Superstition said, "Not me. I want to stay as far away from them as I can. I don't want *that* to get on me!" My response was something like, "What? You mean you think *that* can get on you?" Superstition believed, whether demon or attitude, it could spread to her like a virus. Sure, the lady was uncomfortable, but she didn't have a demon. I was astonished at Superstition's reaction. Even if a demon was involved, Superstition's lack of understanding that Christ is in us and of the authority He has given to us was apparent.

Jesus didn't have this attitude. In view of the NT, neither is it the reaction of a Holy Spirit filled child of God. Consider the sons of Sceva in Acts 19:13-17. The demon(s) they encountered beat and stripped them. But the sons of Sceva didn't know the Lord. They addressed the demons in the "Name of Jesus who Paul preaches." But we know the Lord. We are children of the living God. He has filled us with His Spirit and has given us His word. Come on now, who are we! More than that — who is He who lives inside us? Of course demons can attack us, and attack us they do, but we have authority over them through the Name of Jesus. We are more than conquerors through Him who loves us.

Chapter 1

The Gospels

Jesus, People, and the Enemy

The Gospels: New Covenant or Old?

As a foundation, it is essential to understand the people in the Gospels were still under the Old Covenant. Jesus had not yet died. The New Covenant was not yet purchased by His blood during the Gospels.

The New Covenant is not enacted until after Jesus' death: *For where a covenant is, there must of necessity be the death of the one who made it. 17 For a covenant is valid only when men are dead, for it is never in force while the one who made it lives (Hebrews 9:16-17).* Furthermore John states: *But this He [Jesus] spoke of the Spirit, whom those who believed in Him were to receive; for the Spirit was not yet given, because Jesus was not yet glorified (John 7:39).* And according to Romans 8:9 if someone doesn't have the Spirit he doesn't belong to Christ: *However, you are not in the flesh but in the Spirit, if indeed the Spirit of God dwells in you. But if anyone does not have the Spirit of Christ, he does not belong to Him.* Jesus' death made the New Covenant available and the Holy Spirit's regenerating indwelling makes someone born again.

It is essential to have the Spirit in order to belong to Christ. Were the people in the Gospels followers? Yes. Were they born again? No, not until after the death of the Testator, Jesus Christ. Jesus first had to die for the New Covenant to be available. Therefore none of the people in the Gospels who had demons cast out of them were born again. They did not have the Holy Spirit living inside them. So, yes, people who are not born again can have a demon cast out of them. But it is impossible, because of the above scriptures that any of the people in the Gospels that had a demon driven out of them were born again. Jesus makes this distinction concerning John the Baptist: *"Truly I say to you, among those born of women there has not arisen anyone greater than John the Baptist! Yet the one who is least in the kingdom of heaven is greater than he"* (Matthew 11:11). And: *"The Law and the Prophets were proclaimed until John; since that time the gospel of the kingdom of God has been preached, and everyone is forcing his way into it"* (Luke 16:16). John was the greatest of the OT prophets, but he was not part of the kingdom. John died before Jesus' death and resurrection.

Jesus Explains Demonic Activity INSIDE a Person

With this in mind, Jesus says this about someone who is inhabited by a demon and the activity of that demon:

> *And He [Jesus] was casting out a demon, and it was mute; when the demon had gone out, the mute man spoke; and the crowds were amazed. 15 But some of them said, "He casts out demons by Beelzebul, the ruler of the demons." 16 Others, to test Him, were demanding of Him a sign from heaven. 17 But He knew their thoughts and said to them, "Any kingdom divided against itself is laid waste; and a house divided against itself falls. 18 "If Satan also is divided against himself, how will his kingdom stand? For you say that I cast out demons by Beelzebul. 19 And if I by Beelzebul cast out demons, by whom do your sons cast them out? So they will be your judges. 20 But if I cast out demons by the finger of God, then the kingdom of God has come upon you."*
>
> Luke 11:14-26

Matthew adds Jesus' significant statement: *"Or how can anyone enter the strong man's house and carry off his property, unless he first binds the strong man? And then he will plunder his house"* (Matthew 12:29).

Continuing in Luke:

> *"21 When a strong man, fully armed, guards his own house, his possessions are undisturbed. 22 But when someone stronger than he attacks him and overpowers him, he takes away from him all his armor on which he had relied and distributes his plunder. 23 He who is not with Me is against Me; and he who does not gather with Me, scatters. 24 When the unclean spirit goes out of a man, it passes through*

waterless places seeking rest, and not finding any, it says, 'I will return to my house from which I came.' 25 And when it comes, it finds it swept and put in order. 26 Then it goes and takes along seven other spirits more evil than itself, and they go in and live there; and the last state of that man becomes worse than the first."

Luke 11:21-26

To understand this passage we must identify:
- Who is the strong man?
- Who is the stronger than he?
- What is the house?
- What is fully armed?
- What is the armor?
- What is the plunder—the possessions?
- What is the meaning of verse 23 in its context?

Examining the words "strong man," "stronger," and "house" let's look at a couple scenarios. Recall, in context, Jesus is talking about demons inside people. First, let's look at replacing God for the strong man and a demon for the stronger. The house is a person according to verse 24; whether body, soul, or spirit won't matter for this discussion. It will be revisited later. With these insertions, Luke 11:21-22 would read like this: "When God, fully armed, guards His own person, His possessions are undisturbed. 22 But when a demon stronger than God attacks God and overpowers God, that devil takes away from God all God's armor on which God had relied and distributes his [the demon's] plunder."

Immediately we can see this does not work, for who is stronger than God? Now we try replacing a demon for the strong man and God for the stronger. Luke 11:21-22 reads: "When a demon, fully armed, guards his own person, that demon's possessions are undisturbed. 22 But when God stronger than that demon attacks that demon and overpowers him, God takes away from that demon all that demon's armor on which that demon had relied and God distributes His plunder." That works.

Looking again at Matthew 12:29 with God for stronger, demon for strong, and person for house, it would read like this: "Or how can God enter the demon's person and carry off the demon's property, unless God first binds the demon? And then God will plunder the demon's person."

From OT examples, to plunder and divide the spoil was to take by force for one's self what used to belong to someone else. Israel often plundered others, taking their stuff for their own. Remember, in this section of scripture, Jesus is talking about one person and demonic invasion within that one person. Demonic inhabitation. Context must be emphasized lest people draw from Luke 11 support for anything beyond Jesus' intent.

Jesus continues by issuing a warning: a person who has had a demon driven out of them by the Spirit of God will end up in worse shape, if they don't receive Jesus and so become inhabited by the Holy Spirit. Note the house gets swept and put in order, but is still unoccupied. We can see from verse 24 the restlessness of demonic spirits. They want a house: a habitation. Their resolve is to live inside of people. The Greek Lexicon's word for "house" in verse 21 is αὐλή. It is defined as: "…an uncovered space around the house, enclosed by a wall; house or palace; the uncovered courtyard of the house. In the OT particularly of the courts of the tabernacle and of the temple in Jerusalem." This is quite telling. Many who claim a demon can live inside a believer are also emphatic they can live in the soul or flesh, even if they cannot live in their spirit. Their proof text is Paul's thorn in the flesh (2 Corinthians 12:7). They relate it to their understanding surrounding the Temple's outer courts. But here the word "house" is broader than the inside. It is far more inclusive, since it not only refers to the inner house, but the outer courts, as well.

Now let's take a second look at these scriptures in Luke 11:

"When a strong man, fully armed, guards his own house, his possessions are undisturbed." (22)

When a demon lives inside a person, and through its deception, bondage, and lies, (his armor) he builds a fortress around his person, he keeps his person imprisoned to him; he is unprovoked and unchallenged as master and his authority over his person remains.

"But when someone stronger than he attacks him and overpowers him, he takes away from him all his armor on which he had relied and distributes his plunder." (22)

But, when the Holy Spirit Who is stronger than the demon attacks that demon and overpowers (Greek: to conquer) him, He reveals to the person all the deception, bondage, and lies (the armor; weapons) the demon was relying upon to keep them imprisoned to him. Then God sets the person free from the demon's prison, delivering them and giving them back control of their life. ("Distributes" means "to give over, deliver," therefore "distribute his plunder" means that God delivered the person and gave them back control of their life.) The person is free and has regained control of their life. But verse 23 issues a warning to this freed person:

> "He who is not with Me is against Me; and he who does not gather with Me, scatters." (23)

However, if the freed person doesn't want to come to Jesus and gather with Him after they have been delivered from the demon, then this person will be scattered. Scattered (GL): "of those who, routed or terror stricken or driven by some other impulses, fly in every direction." Scattering is the result of not gathering with Jesus. What is meant by scattering? The thought continues with verse 24:

> "When the unclean spirit goes out of a man, it passes through waterless places seeking rest, and not finding any, it says, 'I will return to my house from which I came.'" (24)

Verse 24 does not say the Holy Spirit was involved in the unclean spirit leaving. There are, therefore, two different ways of understanding this scripture. They both have the same outcome, so I will point out the differences, but not emphasize them:

1. The devil may have been driven out by the Holy Spirit. But afterward the individual did not receive Jesus. They, therefore, did not receive the indwelling Holy Spirit. The person remained unoccupied. This appears to be the correct understanding in view of verse 22-23.

2. The demon may have had open-door access to his person to come and go at will. Clearly we can see from the scriptures that demons can seize their subjects. They seize them, throw them into fire or water, trying to kill them (Mk 9:18-27). While at other times their activity seems

somewhat dormant. In these situations, is the demon coming and going or just dormant or active? We don't know from scripture.

In this scenario, however, the devil came out and now is roaming around looking for another habitation of rest. When it didn't find rest the demon purposed to come back to its first house (the person):

"And when it comes, it finds it swept and put in order." (25)

When the demon comes back, it finds the place (the person) cleaned up and put in order. This means the person had returned to health—relieved of torment, returned to sanity, recovered from a demon-induced ailment, gotten their life in order, etc. The Bible teaches demons can make people mentally and physically ill. We may conclude that if a demon was making someone mentally or physically ill, when the demon left then the person could[1] recover. Jesus' main point, however, was that the place, the person, was left unoccupied:

"Then it goes and takes along seven other spirits more evil than itself, and they go in and live there; and the last state of that man becomes worse than the first." (26)

Left unoccupied, the demon returns to its person with seven worse demons. They not only haunt the person—they inhabit them. Furthermore, though Jesus didn't elaborate, bringing the seven worse spirits upon returning was likely for stronger alliances. Seeing it wasn't able to destroy the person on its own, the first demon sought out demons worse than itself to complete the demolition. And since the number is seven, the number of completion, it probably means the destruction of the person this time was complete and final. To reiterate: the devil left, came back, and found the place unoccupied and cleaned. It then left to round up reinforcements. Upon their arrival they found the person unoccupied and cleaned up. They reestablish habitation—bringing hell with them.

---

[1] "Could" because often people need physical and/or mental healing. Some do not. Demons want to destroy people. As people continually believe demons' lies these lies become part of the person. They change their thoughts, outlook, and worldview. Their minds must be renewed and possibly healed. Physical destruction from demons' influence is the same. Some receive healing with their deliverance, some do not.

One final word when encountering demons within an unbeliever: be led by the Holy Spirit and use caution. If the demon-possessed doesn't want Jesus, according to this text in Luke, they will likely end up in a worse state. Nowhere in the Bible is a demon able to keep someone from coming to Jesus. Even in the case of Legion (Mark 5:6), the person still had free choice to come to Jesus. In fact he ran to Him and bowed before Him.

This section of scripture clearly demonstrates that if a demon is present, God first kicks it out before He enters. People who want to promote that demons can be within a Christian don't like to hear this, but it is God's Word. God does not live side-by-side with a demon in His temple. No, He binds the demon, conquers it, and delivers the person.

Jesus and Satan

Since Jesus is our ultimate example, what were Satan's tactics and how did Jesus handle him?

God talks little about Satan in scripture. But where He does we can acquire great insight on how Satan works, his motives, his tactics, and subsequently, his allies. In the Gospels there are a few times when Jesus interacted with Satan himself. However, many believers think about, focus on, and talk about him far too much. Since God talks little about Satan we should too.

Some characteristics are clearly satanic. And since the heart of the un-regenerated person is desperately wicked, Satan's ways and thoughts are easily cultivated in soil of their hearts. As we read through history it is easy to see where Satan and his ways meet with the wicked hearts of men. Herod the Great and Pharaoh were such men.

Satan is a killer. Immediately, upon the news that Mary was pregnant, Satan sought to kill Jesus. God had never been vulnerable. But now as a fetus He was. What is more vulnerable than a fetus? Satan knew he must stop the plan of God. Messiah on the scene meant his downfall. He knew it. He knew this meant that mankind would have another opportunity to reign. Man had forfeited that right and he knew it. Reigning was his ambition, his destiny, his determination. He knew Messiah ultimately meant his imprisonment (Revelation 20:2), the Kingdom of God established on the Earth, and his final destiny—the Lake of Fire—forever. So, he enticed Herod to kill all the babies that could possibly be around Jesus' age. Messiah Jesus lived. Satan failed.

Satan kills to get his way. He kills to control. He kills, because killing is his nature. He is a murderer. And he influences people to do his work and promote his ways. But God warned Mary and Joseph guiding them away from danger.

Matthew 4 is the first time Satan is specifically mentioned in the Gospels. He is confronting Jesus face-to-face. Matthew 4:1-11 identifies him as Satan, the devil, and the tempter. Each of these words describes our enemy. Let's look at the definitions from the Greek Lexicon as he is the personification of each.

- Devil: a calumniator, false accuser, and slanderer.
- Tempter: to try whether a thing can be done; to attempt, endeavor, to try, make trial of, test: for the purpose of ascertaining his quality, or what he thinks, or how he will behave himself; to test one maliciously, craftily to put to the proof his feelings or judgments; to try or test one's faith, virtue, character, by enticement to sin; to solicit to sin, to tempt.
- Satan: adversary (one who opposes another in purpose or act), the name given to the prince of evil spirits—the inveterate adversary of God and Christ.

Now let's go back to Matthew 4. Realize that as Satan dealt with Jesus he will deal with us and every other person. *"If You are the Son of God, command that these stones become bread,"* said the Tempter (Matthew 4:3). Satan comes to Jesus when Jesus' body is at its weakest, after He had been fasting 40 days. Satan chose that time. His nature is to prey on the weak. He doesn't care if we are in mental anguish from the death of a loved one or if we are sick in the hospital or dying; he will attack us whenever he can—whenever there is an opportunity. He has no empathy, no pity, no mercy, and no kindness.

Tempter (Satan) first tempts Jesus in His area of need. He knew Jesus was hungry and weak from fasting. Tempter attempted to move Jesus to misuse His power and His anointing by providing for His immediate need. He was indeed the Son of God and could command those stone to become bread; Jesus could prove to His adversary that He was indeed the one and only Son of God. But He didn't.

Jesus not only was and is the Son of God, He is also the Bread of Life. Jesus knew He could make bread appear, after all He had done it many times—6 days a week for 40 years (Exodus 16:35). Satan knew it too. Satan used scripture, howbeit incorrectly; he implied the first part of Deuteronomy 8:3. But, Jesus knew Deuteronomy 8:3, He was there. He wrote it. He is the Word of God. He knew the connection between those 40 years and His 40 days: *"It is written,"* He rebutted, *"Man shall not live by bread alone, but by every word that proceeds from the mouth of God."*

Do we hear Tempter? Tempter attacks our identity too. He challenges our identity as children of God, our calling, our gifts, our relationships—he attacks anything he can. The thoughts sound so normal—so natural to our way of thinking. They sound like us. They sound like the person down the street or at the barn. They sound so believable. Don't believe them. They are lies from the pit of hell.

Tempter will temp us, then accuse us of thinking the thought when the thought was his planting—his whisper. The thought is not sin; temptation is not sin; Jesus was tempted. How we respond is what matters. It is what determines whether we enter into sin or not. How often are we inspired by the enemy to misuse our influence and anointing to promote ourselves or to get what we want? Jesus never misused His power—never.

Our ability to recall scriptures, as Jesus did, is of incomparably great value. Tempter twists truth. He is an expert. The original temptation in Eden was exactly that—twisting what God had actually said. Furthermore, "word" in Matthew 4:4: *"every word that proceeds out of the mouth of God"* is "rhema" not "logos," illuminating our need to hear God in the moment and not to just quote a scripture. Jesus didn't just quote a scripture, He quoted the right scripture as led by the Holy Spirit. This is vividly expressed in the next temptation:

> *Then the devil took Him into the holy city and had Him stand on the pinnacle of the temple, 6 and said to Him, "If You are the Son of God, throw Yourself down; for it is written, 'He will command His angels concerning You'; and 'on their hands they will bear You up, so that You will not strike Your foot against a stone.'" 7 Jesus said to him, "On the other hand, it is written, 'you shall not put the LORD your God to the test.'"*
>
> *Matthew 4:5-7*

Drawing from Psalm 91, the devil tried again to entice Jesus into proving He was the Son of God. "If You are...then..." Jesus, instead of addressing Psalm 91, speaks directly to the intent of the devil. He fetches the rhema word from Deuteronomy 6, and with an *"It is written..."* He demolishes the devil's presumptuous attempt. Jesus was not out to prove anything. He knew who He was and why He came. God came to serve; God came to die.

How about you?

Are you out to prove your greatness?

> *Again, the devil took Him to a very high mountain and showed Him all the kingdoms of the world and their glory; 9 and he said to Him, "All these things I will give You, if You fall down and worship me." 10 Then Jesus said to him, "Go, Satan! For it is written, 'You shall worship the LORD your God, and serve Him only.'"*
>
> *Matthew 4:8-10*

Surely the devil had read Psalm 2:7-8, hadn't he? *"7 I will surely tell of the decree of the LORD: He said to Me, 'You are My Son, Today I have begotten You. 8 Ask of Me, and I will surely give the nations as Your inheritance, And the very ends of the earth as Your possession."*

The nations were already Jesus' inheritance, as the Father had decreed. Jesus was already inheriting the nations, just not Satan's way. After all, God had now become a man; could Satan get Jesus to tap into the lust for power that many men before had bowed to? This is the first of many times in the Gospels where Jesus owns the conversation. He speaks to the enemy on His own terms and not on the devil's. He doesn't even address His inheritance, rather He pinpoints Satan's ultimate hunger—worship. The antichrist, Satan's habitation in Revelation, demands worship. Dissenting holds the penalty of death. That is the issue here. Instead Jesus goes directly to the heart of man's existence: worship and service. Who or what will we worship? Who or what will we serve?

Satan has many tactics. The following is from my blog: http://soaringintheprophetic.blogspot.com

Satan is a Community Organizer

How was it that Jesus was finally put to death? Not by what means, as in the Cross and the nails, but rather why did the people kill their Messiah King? What set the stage for such a diabolical rage of the masses?

From the time of Jesus' birth Satan wanted this One—this Only Begotten—DEAD! It seems obvious Satan is who incited Herod to kill all the babies around Jesus' age. Thus his evil pursuit began right after Jesus was born. Nevertheless, Jesus escaped due to his parents' prophetic revelations from God. First to Egypt, then to Galilee. Later Satan tempted Jesus in the desert trying to gain His allegiance through intrigue, but to no avail.

We know Jesus laid down His own life, but what was Satan's part? How did Satan finally accomplish his evil scheme? Besides his brief appearance in the desert, while Jesus was fasting, the Bible doesn't say much about what the enemy was doing between the birth and death of Jesus. So what was he up to? I think he was community organizing!

Satan worked through the masses—the people. He knows the heart of man apart from God. He knows it is desperately wicked, so they would be his pawns, his puppets—his ignorant allies. He waged war through their thoughts, religion, jealousy, and through deception. He worked by enticing the soul of man. Man at his worst. Man's twisted evil unregenerate soul. Then he gave them a channel through which their anger and hatred could flow. That is how Satan worked out his evil scheme. He thought, "I can't kill Him so I will incite others to do it for me. I will use their system, their framework, and their laws … their evil hearts will bow to me. They will do it for me! Yes, that will work." And it did.

This community organizer's intrigue is on the rise again with increasingly intense acceleration. He is stirring up the masses by inciting hatred, flaring racial tensions, social tensions, religious tensions, and economic tensions. He is breaking down the doors wherever sin has been crouching. With every opportunity he is ravaging our streets—in our America, in our world.

But what did the Lord say? *"When the enemy comes in like a flood, The Spirit of the LORD will lift up a standard against him."* God is a community organizer too.

Jesus, His Disciples, and Demons

To reiterate, Book 2 discusses winds of doctrine that teach demons can dwell within a Christian—someone born of His Spirit. Therefore this section will not be an exhaustive discourse on every encounter Jesus and His disciples had with demons. Many books have been written about that subject. My goal is to show from the scriptures that a demon cannot reside within a Christian.

But He [Jesus] answered and said, "I was sent only to the lost sheep of the house of Israel" (Matthew 15:24). Jesus was sent only to the lost sheep of the house of Israel and that is where He sent His disciples too.

> *These twelve Jesus sent out after instructing them: "Do not go in the way of the Gentiles, and do not enter any city of the Samaritans; 6 but rather go to the lost sheep of the house of Israel. 7 And as you go, preach, saying, 'The kingdom of heaven is at hand.'"*
>
> *(Matthew 10:5-7)*

"Lost sheep" means they were lost. They were not Christians indwelt by the Holy Spirit, since Jesus had not yet died, purchasing our salvation.

Matthew 10:6 is not all inclusive, however Matthew 15:24 is. Meaning, Matthew 10:6 is a single event, whereas Matthew 15:24 contains the word "only." All people in the Gospels were lost, meaning unsaved, but not all were lost sheep of the house of Israel. Jesus spent little time preaching outside these lost sheep: The woman of Canaan (Matthew 15) and the woman from Samaria (John 4), are two examples where He did.

Although demons are subject to us, we should not make that our focus:

> *"The seventy returned with joy, saying, "Lord, even the demons are subject to us in Your name." 18 And He said to them, "I was watching Satan fall from heaven like lightning. 19 Behold, I have given you authority to tread on serpents and scorpions, and over all the power of the enemy, and nothing will injure you. 20 Nevertheless do not rejoice in this, that the spirits are subject to you, but rejoice that your names are recorded in heaven."*
>
> *Luke 10:17-20*

Why then do so many Christians focus on the devil and demons? We should emphasize and focus on what God says we should. It seems that those who talk a lot about the enemy often encounter him in unusual measure. The enemy appears to hang around those who focus on him. He is a narcissist, pining away lustfully at his own reflection. When Jesus and His disciples encountered demons they weren't looking for them. They didn't stand on mountain tops making declarations into the atmosphere breaking strongholds and addressing principalities. The NT emphasis is far different. They dealt with the devil and demons as they encountered them. Chapter 4: Truth in Tension will discuss this subject further.

Judas and Satan

Satan entered Judas during communion at the Last Supper. Can you imagine Jesus sitting across from Judas at the Last Supper knowing full well what was about to take place? And then as Satan entered Judas right in front of Him? Here are things we know about Judas:

- Judas was a thief, yet Jesus had him carry the money bag. (John 13:29) I wonder if it was to give him every opportunity to repent.
- Judas was called a devil by Jesus. (John 6:70)
- Judas betrayed Jesus. (Matthew 10:4)
- Judas was an apostle, chosen by God—ponder that one!
- Jesus hung around with him.
- Not one of the apostles knew or considered Judas was the betrayer; he must have looked and acted just like they did. (John 13:25-30)
- Judas went to hell. (Mark 14:21) He was remorseful for his betrayal (Matthew 27:3), but never asked Jesus for forgiveness. We know this because of Matthew 26:24-25.

- Judas never called Jesus Lord.

Though Judas was one of the twelve apostles he never had a change of mind or heart. The word "repent" means a change of mind, not a change of action. However, when a mind is changed, subsequently a change of action follows. Therefore, even as faith without works is dead, so repentance without actions is also dead.

"Judas and the First Communion—Something to Ponder" is from my blog after a discussion with my friend, Byron. It gives some insight into the interaction between Jesus and Judas, and Judas and Satan.

Judas and the First Communion—Something to Ponder
From my blog: http://soaringintheprophetic.blogspot.com/

Sometime ago, Byron, a friend of mine shared a story. It was of a priest who would not serve communion to a person he knew to be steeped in sin and unwilling to repent. This got me thinking about communion. I stated I would not have served communion to this person either, because I know the Bible says:

> Therefore whoever eats the bread or drinks the cup of the Lord in an unworthy manner, shall be guilty of the body and the blood of the Lord. 28 But a man must examine himself, and in so doing he is to eat of the bread and drink of the cup. 29 For he who eats and drinks, eats and drinks judgment to himself if he does not judge the body rightly. 30 For this reason many among you are weak and sick, and a number sleep. 31 But if we judged ourselves rightly, we would not be judged.
>
> *1 Corinthians 11:27-31*

As I considered my position before the Lord, the Lord revealed something to me. Let's look at the very first communion:

> Now before the Feast of the Passover, Jesus knowing that His hour had come that He would depart out of this world to the Father, having loved His own who were in the world, He loved them to the end. 2 During supper, the devil having already put into the heart of Judas Iscariot, the son of Simon, to betray Him, 3 Jesus, knowing that the Father had given all things into His hands, and that He had come forth from God and was going back to God, 4 got up from supper, and laid aside His garments; and taking a towel, He girded Himself. 5 Then He poured water into the basin, and began to wash the disciples' feet and to wipe them with the towel with which He was girded. 6 So He came to Simon Peter. He said to Him, "Lord, do You wash my feet?" 7 Jesus answered and said to him, "What I do you do not realize now, but you will understand hereafter." 8 Peter said to Him, "Never shall You wash my feet!" Jesus answered him, "If I do not wash you, you have no part with Me." 9 Simon Peter said to Him, "Lord, then wash not only my feet, but also my hands and my

head." 10 Jesus said to him, "He who has bathed needs only to wash his feet, but is completely clean; and you are clean, but not all of you." 11 For He knew the one who was betraying Him; for this reason He said, "Not all of you are clean." 12 So when He had washed their feet, and taken His garments and reclined at the table again, He said to them, "Do you know what I have done to you? 13 You call Me Teacher and Lord; and you are right, for so I am. 14 If I then, the Lord and the Teacher, washed your feet, you also ought to wash one another's feet. 15 For I gave you an example that you also should do as I did to you. 16 Truly, truly, I say to you, a slave is not greater than his master, nor is one who is sent greater than the one who sent him. 17 If you know these things, you are blessed if you do them."

18 "I do not speak of all of you. I know the ones I have chosen; but it is that the Scripture may be fulfilled, 'HE WHO EATS MY BREAD HAS LIFTED UP HIS HEEL AGAINST ME.' 19 From now on I am telling you before it comes to pass, so that when it does occur, you may believe that I am He. 20 Truly, truly, I say to you, he who receives whomever I send receives Me; and he who receives Me receives Him who sent Me." 21 When Jesus had said this, He became troubled in spirit, and testified and said, "Truly, truly, I say to you, that one of you will betray Me." 22 The disciples began looking at one another, at a loss to know of which one He was speaking. 23 There was reclining on Jesus' bosom one of His disciples, whom Jesus loved. 24 So Simon Peter gestured to him, and said to him, "Tell us who it is of whom He is speaking." 25 He, leaning back thus on Jesus' bosom, said to Him, "Lord, who is it?"

26 Jesus then answered, "That is the one for whom I shall dip the morsel and give it to him." So when He had dipped the morsel, He took and gave it to Judas, the son of Simon Iscariot. 27 After the morsel, Satan then entered into him. Therefore Jesus said to him, "What you do, do quickly." 28 Now no one of those reclining at the table knew for what purpose He had said this to him. 29 For some were supposing, because Judas had the money box, that Jesus was saying to him, "Buy the things we have need of for the feast"; or else, that he should give something to the poor. 30 So after receiving the morsel he went out immediately; and it was night.

31 Therefore when he had gone out, Jesus said, "Now is the Son of Man glorified, and God is glorified in Him.

John 13

Jesus gave Judas communion. It was at that point Satan entered Judas—right there at the Last Supper during communion as Jesus handed him the bread!! Judas drank judgment upon himself and Jesus not only let him—Jesus offered it to him. I had to adjust my position. Interestingly, at the very first communion Satan was present waiting for an opportunity. Satan knew what he'd sown in Judas' heart. Now at communion—the very first one—Judas, eating and drinking in an unworthy manner, ate and drank judgment upon himself and flung wide open a door, which Satan had prepared earlier in his heart.

Communion is not just a ritual we go through, it is a spiritual experience we have with the Lord whether we feel like it is or not; much more than eating a wafer and drinking something made from grapes is happening. Leaders must warn people when communion is being served, then follow Jesus' example and let everyone choose for themselves.

Chapter 2

Acts and the Epistles

Demons' Aim in Believers' Lives

ARE YOU UNDER THE INFLUENCE of a tactical planner? That, dear reader, is the ardent plan of your enemy. His plan is to influence your every thought, action, and direction. In the first six chapters of Nehemiah, Nehemiah's dealings with Sanballat, Tobiah, and Geshem shed a great deal of light on the devil's tactics against us. The devil and his demons use trickery, craftiness, deceit, mockery, and slander. He even uses things appearing to be good, but things in which God never wanted us to be involved. Demons set traps for us, then lie in wait to see if we will fall into their snare. If not, they wait for a more opportune time using the same tactic or they try new tactics to see what we'll respond to. On and on it goes. Ultimately their goal is to kill us. However, if they can't kill us, they will try anything to stop the work of God in and through us. They use any means to get their purpose accomplished. Their only restraint is God.

In the life of Jesus, Satan used one of Jesus' own disciples (Matthew 16:23) and the scriptures (Matthew 4) against Him, who is the Word. Ironic.

Demons Try to Influence Thinking

Peter didn't realize he has been listening to Satan. But then the devil's words came out his own mouth: *But He [Jesus] turned and said to Peter, "Get behind Me, Satan! You are an offense to Me, for you are not mindful of the things of God, but the things of men" (Matthew 16:23).* Peter "counseled" Jesus according to Satan's whispers and Jesus nailed him for it. Peter, however, did get better discerning the enemy's influence. In Acts 5:3 Peter said: *"Ananias, why has Satan filled your heart to lie to the Holy Spirit?"* Peter recognized the influence of Satan this time.

The devil's goal is to have us and ultimately to kill us. But, if he can't do that, then he wants to control us. His best shot at controlling us is to influence our thinking. Why? If he can affect the way we think then his influence is in every area of our life. Therefore, to the degree which he can influence our beliefs about God, about mankind, our worldview, etc. is the degree to which he can control us—he as the master puppeteer and people as his puppets.

Demons Tempt

Demons tempt. In fact tempter is one of the identities of Satan, as we saw from chapter 1. When he met Jesus in the desert to tempt Him, the Bible calls Satan "the tempter." He tempts all people. 1 John 5:19 says: *We know that we are of God, and that the whole world lies in the power of the evil one.* Most people are ignorant they are under the influence of demons. Often it is ignorance of the devil's strategies that lends to defeat. God says in Hosea 4 that His people are destroyed for lack of knowledge. But we can increase our chances of victory by allowing truth to confront and influence us, instead of using excuses or nostrums.

James 1 reveals the "hook and lure" tactics of our enemy:

> *Let no one say when he is tempted, "I am being tempted by God"; for God cannot be tempted by evil, and He Himself does not tempt anyone. 14 But each one is tempted when he is carried away and enticed by his own lust. 15 Then when lust has conceived, it gives birth to sin; and when sin is accomplished, it brings forth death.*
> *James 1:13-15*

Insightful sequence. Much like picking the perfect fishing spot and bait; the enemy tosses in the lure and line. Will we bite? If we do he reels us in like a fish on a line. If not, he tries another bait. He can't see into our hearts, so he fishes. He's looking for a desire within us. What will attract us so that he can entice and carry us away? He tries over and over. When sinful desires respond in our heart, we have taken the bait. Now we are no longer dealing with a temptation, it has become sin. Once desire conceives and becomes sin it is much harder to overcome, for then sin has grown roots in our heart. Where there is sin, death too is present. We can avoid the full ramifications of sin by stopping its progression through repentance. If we don't repent, sin will mature and bring forth that death. James puts all the responsibility on the person who is being tempted. He says nothing about a demon needing to be cast out first so that victory may follow. He places the responsibility wholly on the person's desire taking the bait. There are times when we must plain endure temptation. The fight is on. It's our choice. A hard one, but still our choice. James shows the process to temptation. Let's look closer at Acts 5 regarding Ananias and Sapphira and identify temptation's process found in James:

> But Peter said, "Ananias, why has Satan filled your heart to lie to the Holy Spirit and to keep back some of the price of the land? 4 While it remained unsold, did it not remain your own? And after it was sold, was it not under your control? Why is it that you have conceived this deed in your heart? You have not lied to men but to God." 5 And as he heard these words, Ananias fell down and breathed his last; and great fear came over all who heard of it.
>
> *Acts 5:3-5*

Acts 5 is an example of Satan's temptation leading to death. Ananias and Sapphira wanted to appear as something they were not. Satan didn't cut a hole into Ananias' heart and fill it with a lie. What, then, is meant by Satan filling a heart to lie? Consider Ananias and Sapphira as they traveled down this road called "Temptation," which led them to death. Here are the steps:

1. There must be a mind open to temptation.
2. An enemy's thought is offered. (the bait; the temptation)
3. The thought is considered. (the bait begins luring leading to enticement)
4. Ownership of the thought is transferred from the enemy to the person. (conception in the heart; the process of death begins; biting the bait)
5. The person begins to ponder how to accomplish their thought. (sin's birth; reeling in)

6.   Action is carried out. (death begins to reign, for sin's payment is always death; the fish is landed)

Temptation comes either from within—our own desires—or from an enemy's luring. Either way there must be a place to set the hook and that place is called desire. But temptation also always come with a choice. Consequently, the battle is always won or lost in the mind.

Sinful Anger's Open Door

Ephesians 4:26-27 has been used as a proof text that demons can live inside Christians. Demons, some believe, find their "topos <5117>"[1] through anger's open door. But is that the intent of these two scriptures? And does the context support that belief? Let's look at Ephesians 4:26-27 in order to excavate correct theology through sound exegesis: *BE ANGRY, AND yet DO NOT SIN; do not let the sun go down on your anger, 27 and do not give the devil an opportunity.*[1]

In context, Ephesians 4:17 through 6:9 are a bunch of short directives on Christian living. They are written to a collective group—a church—not to an individual person. Ephesians 4:26-27 is warning against anger sliding into sin, and then affecting others. Preceding these directives is a deep revelatory download by Paul on the Church, the Five-Fold ministry, the equipping of the saints, and how people within the church are to function and grow together. Paul's point is to hold up and magnify the glorious church, show us how she will grow up, and how we as believers are supposed to act. It is not a proof text on a demon-possessed person.

What then does it mean to give the devil an opportunity? An opportunity for what and to do what? Recall, the backdrop of these 2 scriptures is anger. The sun going down indicates the potential of darkness settling in. We can turn power over to and give an occasion for acting to the devil by allowing sinful anger to fester within us. It then easily spreads to others:

---

[1] Greek Lexicon: 5117 τόπος topos top'-os
1) place, any portion or space marked off, as it were from surrounding space 1a) an inhabited place, as a city, village, district 1b) a place (passage) in a book
2) metaph. 2a) the condition or station held by one in any company or assembly 2b) opportunity, power, occasion for acting

Do not associate with a man given to anger; Or go with a hot-tempered man, 25 Or you will learn his ways And find a snare for yourself (Proverbs 22). Sinful anger never stays inside the angry person—it boils out. As it manifests the enemy will try to propel it. Don't let him; don't give him an opportunity.

Jesus stated that sin comes from the heart:

> *"But the things that proceed out of the mouth come from the heart, and those defile the man. 19 For out of the heart come evil thoughts, murders, adulteries, fornications, thefts, false witness, slanders. 20 These are the things which defile the man; but to eat with unwashed hands does not defile the man."*
>
> *Mathew 15:18-20*

Our heart's soil determines whether or not sin finds a place to grow. When the enemy sees soil suitable for cultivation he'll start planting. Don't be that soil. What is in our heart will inevitably come out our mouth giving opportunity to the devil as it spreads to other people. People who are sinfully angry are pulling up a chair for the devil; they are giving him a place. Ephesians is written to a church, so they would be, in a sense, pulling up a chair in the assembly for the devil. But to conclude that the phrase *"to give place to the devil"* indicates a demon can live inside a Christian's soul or spirit (as opposed to their body) is not sound exegesis. To build a doctrine or ministry based on this scripture as supporting demons within Christians is dangerously wrong. Peter wrote that untaught and unstable people distort hard to understand scriptures to their own destruction. It matters what we believe. And it matters whether we are believing correctly.

Not all anger is sin; God is angry with the wicked every day (Psalm 7:11). Recall Jesus overturning the money changers' tables. However, righteous anger can deteriorate into an opportunity for the enemy, if it is allowed to ferment. That is the point of Ephesians 4:26-27.

Escaping the Snare

Our thinking determines our beliefs and worldview, as discussed previously. Paul writes to Timothy about this truth, however, he approaches it from another angle:

> *The Lord's bond-servant must not be quarrelsome, but be kind to all, able to teach, patient when wronged, 25 with gentleness correcting those who are in opposition, if perhaps God may grant them repentance leading to the knowledge of the truth, 26 and they may come to their senses and escape from the snare of the devil, having been held captive by him to do his will.*
>
> 2 Timothy 2:24-26

The devil caught someone in his trap. They became his captive by believing his lie. Believing his lie creates their prison; a prison of opposition to the truth. The key to their prison door comes in the form of someone speaking truth. In order to be set free the captive must receive the truth, which unlocks the prison door. That is the picture painted by 2 Timothy 2:24-26. We are to correct the captive, gently and humbly, hoping they will repent (change their mind). Believing the truth (the Greek means "precise and correct knowledge") overpowers and replaces the lie. They therefore come to their senses and escape the devil's trap. The wording reveals the Holy Spirit is involved, for it is God granting them repentance.

Imprisoned by a Paradigm

John 8 is a classic example of Jesus trying to set people free with the truth. He is going back and forth with the Jews, trying to jar them into seeing that He is Messiah and has come to set them free. Yet, they remain imprisoned by their paradigm. (They should have known, by the prophetic writings, especially Daniel, the exact time of His coming.) Jesus said:

> *"If you continue in My word, then you are truly disciples of Mine; 32 and you will know the truth, and the truth will make you free." 33 They answered Him, "We are Abraham's descendants and have never yet been enslaved to anyone; how is it that You say, 'You will become free'?" 34 Truly, truly, I say to you, everyone who commits sin is the slave of sin. 35 The slave does not remain in the house forever; the son does remain forever. 36 So if the Son makes you free, you will be free indeed."*
>
> John 8:31-36

Jews were in bondage, bound by their jealousy and misunderstanding of the scriptures regarding Messiah. Thinking they were free (because they were Abraham's descendants) kept them from receiving the Truth incarnate and truly becoming free. Sometimes it's the devil who is actively involved in stealing the word sown in a heart; other times he is not. The religious leaders were their own worst enemies. Jesus so articulately said: *"BUT IN VAIN DO THEY WORSHIP ME, TEACHING AS DOCTRINES THE PRECEPTS OF MEN. Neglecting the commandment of God, you hold to the tradition of men" (Mark 7:7-8).* Some hold on to traditions rather than receiving truth just like the Pharisees did.

Satan Lurks in Unforgiveness

Unforgiveness is a bad garden. People who refuse to forgive are setting a scenario for a demonic ambush on both themselves and for the unforgiven. In 2 Corinthians we find this precise situation:

> *Sufficient for such a one is this punishment which was inflicted by the majority, 7 so that on the contrary you should rather forgive and comfort him, otherwise such a one might be overwhelmed by excessive sorrow. 8 Wherefore I urge you to reaffirm your love for him. 9 For to this end also I wrote, so that I might put you to the test, whether you are obedient in all things. 10 But one whom you forgive anything, I forgive also; for indeed what I have forgiven, if I have forgiven anything, I did it for your sakes in the presence of Christ, 11 so that no advantage would be taken of us by Satan, for we are not ignorant of his schemes.*
>
> *2 Corinthians 2:6-11*

Unforgiveness opens an opportunity for the devil to plant in our garden. The man about whom this scripture was written had been involved in sexual sin and had now repented. Paul explains the man could be in danger if too much discipline was exercised. He could be overcome with too much sorrow. And in such a situation the devil could take advantage. Paul exhorts that it was now necessary to make sure this man knew he was received and loved. Otherwise, Satan could take advantage in the situation. People who have committed sins resulting in discipline from church government, who then repent, need an extravagant display of love and acceptance. Church discipline is good, if it is used for good. Its purpose is to bring about godly sorrow leading to repentance and restoration. That is the goal:

> *I now rejoice, not that you were made sorrowful, but that you were made sorrowful to the point of repentance; for you were made sorrowful according to the will of God, so that you might not suffer loss in anything through us. 10 For the sorrow that is according to the will of God produces a repentance without regret, leading to salvation, but the sorrow of the world produces death.*
>
> 2 Corinthians 7:9-10

Note that Paul says: *"sorrowful to the point of repentance… according to the will of God."* But carried too far, discipline leads to an opportunity for Satan.

Our Mind is a Battlefield

It has been said the greatest battlefield of all time is the mind. Though I consider the Cross that battlefield, the point is still well taken. Proverbs 16:32 says: *He who is slow to anger is better than the mighty, And he who rules his spirit, than he who captures a city.* The mind is an intense frontline war zone. Who could possibly conquer it without the help of the Holy Spirit?

> *For though we walk in the flesh, we do not war according to the flesh, 4 for the weapons of our warfare are not of the flesh, but divinely powerful for the destruction of fortresses. 5 We are destroying speculations and every lofty thing raised up against the knowledge of God, and we are taking every thought captive to the obedience of Christ, 6 and we are ready to punish all disobedience, whenever your obedience is complete.*
>
> 2 Corinthians 10:3-6

Forcing our thoughts to obey Christ is spiritual warfare. But how do we know what or how we should think? Remember, as we learned from Acts 5, not all our thoughts are our own. That is an intense reality. The Bible has clear instructions on how to think to please God. A mind that is forced into biblically trained thinking is a mind that will lead to victorious living and a life at peace among the community of like-minded believers. However, reading Revelation 2-3 it is obvious even Jesus doesn't get along with all church communities.

Philippians 4:8 teaches us: *Finally, brethren, whatever is true, whatever is honorable, whatever is right, whatever is pure, whatever is lovely, whatever is of good repute, if there is any excellence and if anything worthy of praise, dwell on these things.* Thinking this way bears good fruit. It means we don't build imaginary scenarios in our minds. We simply dwell on what is true.

But the enemy doesn't want us to think about what is true, honorable, and right. He wants to destroy relationships and lives. He wants to isolate people and fill their minds with lies and mistrust. He wants to keep us in doubt and unbelief. He tries to keep us from church, from reading the Bible, prayer, and anything helpful to our walk with God. How does he do all this? By getting us to believe lies about God, our brothers and sisters in the kingdom, our spouse, even about ourselves; he wants us to believe lies! If God values something, the devil wants it destroyed. Right thinking leads to personal victory and Kingdom values. Wrong thinking leads to defeat, sin, and ultimately death, in one form or another.

The enemy's influence upon our thinking is again Paul's concern in 2 Corinthians 11:3. Listen to Paul as he is moved by the Holy Spirit to issue this warning: *But I am afraid that, as the serpent deceived Eve by his craftiness* [cunning into a specious or false wisdom], *your minds will be led astray from the simplicity and purity of devotion to Christ.* Eve was diabolically influenced by the serpent in the Garden. Satan's lies coiled the character of God and the identity of man. "You can be like God. Just eat this fruit. God is keeping it from you. He isn't really good after all. He lied to you." How often is this the exact temptation in our own thinking? A lie whispered by the whisperer.

But, God is good and He loves us. That is the truth. We must believe it. And when we don't, we must force our minds to believe it anyway. How easily the pitiful whispers become so dominant in our minds. They, as 2 Corinthians 10 says, build, if we allow, fortresses in our thinking—strongholds of resistance—built and forged by the enemy: lies, deception, and death. We must take control. Submit to God in our mind. We have control over our thinking. It's a lie to believe we don't.[1] Many times it

---

[1] This is concerning the normal Christian life. Some people are mentally ill and need medical help to control their minds. Some even with treatment remain ill.

doesn't seem like we do, but we do. We can take our thoughts captive and force them into Kingdom thinking by the power of the Holy Spirit Who lives inside us.

Whose Side are We On?

> Then I heard a loud voice in heaven, saying, "Now the salvation, and the power, and the kingdom of our God and the authority of His Christ have come, for the accuser of our brethren has been thrown down, he who accuses them before our God day and night."
>
> Revelation 12:10

Don't do the devil's work for him standing as an accuser of your fellow Christians. Howbeit, this does not mean we abandon righteous judgment. 1 Corinthians 2:15 says that: *he who is spiritual appraises all things*. Appraises means, "examine or judge; to judge of, estimate, determine (the excellence or defects of any person or thing"; so we are to evaluate all things as spiritually mature people, but not be guilty of pointing the judgmental finger. Church discipline, as discussed in Corinthians, was redemptive in nature. The goal was restoration for the immoral man, to both to God and the church community (1 Corinthians 5). Likewise, our judgments are to be spiritual and, if possible, redemptive. Isaiah prophesied that Jesus would not judge by the sight of His eyes, nor decide by the hearing of His ears; but with righteousness He would judge (Isaiah 11). This is how we too are to evaluate and make judgments.

Chapter 3

---✦ ✝ ✦---

If Not That, Then What?

The New Testament's Perspective

ONE DAY I WALKED INTO CHURCH to hear a friend of mine yelling—no screaming at the top of his lungs. He was in a "deliverance" appointment. My friend had an enormous anger problem. This appointment was intended to get him delivered from it—his anger—which had to be a demon, right? Delivered, because it had to be a demon, since he had it and he had tried to get rid of it, but he still had it, so it had to be a demon. But, even after the screaming and yelling, he still had it—his anger that is. Though demons can influence Christians, deliverance, in this case, was not the right approach. Galatians 5 says that anger is a work of the flesh. If, therefore, a demon is "riding on" a sin originating in the flesh, Christians must themselves take authority over it. As wise woman I know put it, "You cannot cast out the flesh." (Debbie Powell)

One early morning I awoke to friend's voice on the phone. My friend had been awakened in the middle of the night by demons. This person had become a Christian years previous and then had backslidden. In their backslidden years their lifestyle had become very dark. Now God had put me in their life. They had visited church the day before and now, before etiquette would approve, they were on the phone. Why? They had been awakened in the night by three demons hovering over their bed. As my friend looked at each of them they could see pieces of their darkened personality in each: one lust; one fear; one addiction. They explained that they pleaded with Jesus to get rid of them as they peeked out from under their blankets. But Jesus' response was that He would not; instead, they were to use His name to get rid of them. Peeping out from under their blankets they pointed to the first one, "In Jesus name get out of here!" Poof—gone. Then to the second one, "In Jesus name." Poof—gone. The third one boasted in pomp, "I don't have to leave and you cannot make me!" Jesus again told her to use His name. Pointing her little finger out from her blankets, "In Jesus name leave!" Poof—gone! It was at this point my friend called me. Their backsliding had taken them to where demons tread. They had allowed demons to influence their mind to such an overwhelming degree demons had become part of their personality. Not because they lived inside of my friend, rather because my friend had given in to their temptation so many times, their temptations had become my friend's way of thinking: their mindset; their worldview; their personality. Now having been set free from them, my friend needed to renew their mind; they needed to learn to think differently. For though they were free from the demons, they were not free from their own way of thinking, which they had learned from the demons. Furthermore, though they were freed from the demons, there was no guarantee they would stay away. In fact, the testimony of Scripture is that they would not. They would be back in force looking for an opportunity to once again find their way into my friend's way of thinking and life. Sadly, years later they did. Small cracks finally gave way to an open door: an opportunity.

The world, the flesh, and the devil are all our enemies (1 John 2:16, Galatians 5:17, 1 Peter 5:8 respectively). Many problems in our life may simply be our fleshly nature hindering us, after all it tutored us all the years we lived without God. Or it may be worldliness—loving the world and what it offers more than God: His ways and His Kingdom. Or perhaps it is a demon whispering in our ear intending to influence our emotions and thus our actions.

Concerning our enemies: the world, the flesh, and the devil, what does the NT say about overcoming them? As we consider the answer to this question, remember the epistles are written to either churches or to individual Christians. It is interesting to contemplate on why none of the epistles (Romans –Jude) mention anything about demon expulsion. Exorcism was obvious in the Gospels and Acts, and still should be practiced by believers towards unbelievers who have a demon within them (see Mark 16:17-20). The reason for the silence in the epistles speaks volumes; the sound of silence, so to speak. Let me explain. The Corinthians had a mess of a church. Paul corrected them on many issues ranging from a lack of forgiveness, to spiritual gifts, communion, sexual sin, and excommunication from the church. However, not a word was mentioned about their practice of demon exorcism. Interesting. Why? Could it be because within the church (the people of God) exorcism didn't take place? If this was the case it would explain the silence. Let's walk through the epistles to discover what the NT emphasizes.

Walk by the Spirit

There is a war going on inside of us. The Spirit of God and our flesh are opposed to each other. Both want to be [L]lord and both want the throne of our heart. That is a problem.

> *But I say, walk by the Spirit, and you will not carry out the desire of the flesh. 17 For the flesh sets its desire against the Spirit, and the Spirit against the flesh; for these are in opposition to one another, so that you may not do the things that you please. 18 But if you are led by the Spirit, you are not under the Law. 19 Now the deeds of the flesh are evident, which are: immorality, impurity, sensuality, 20 idolatry, sorcery, enmities, strife, jealousy, outbursts of anger, disputes, dissensions, factions, 21 envying, drunkenness, carousing, and things like these, of which I forewarn you, just as I have forewarned you, that those who practice such things will not inherit the kingdom of God.*
>
> *Galatians 5:16-21*

Read again verses 19-21; those are the works of the flesh. It is the flesh that displays these characteristics. Jamieson, Fausset, Brown Commentary discusses the flesh this way: "the natural man, out of which flow the evils specified (#Ga 5:19-21). The spirit and the flesh mutually exclude one another. It is promised, not that we should have no evil lusts, but that we should "not *fulfill*" them. If the spirit that is in us can be at ease under sin, it is not a spirit that comes from the Holy Spirit. The gentle dove trembles at the sight even of a hawk's feather." If we are comfortable with fleshly ways mentioned in Galatians 5, then we are living in grave deception.

Galatians 5:18 states: *But if you are led by the Spirit, you are not under the Law.* The word for Law is νόμος. Most translations do not capitalize law. It can refer to the Mosaic Law or it can be "anything established, anything received by usage, a custom, a law, a command (Greek Lexicon)." The depths of Galatians 5:18 is enormous; it's themed throughout the NT. In fact, the Sermon on the Mount echoes its sentiments (Matthew 5-7), for who can live Jesus' words contained within unless he is led by the Holy Spirit? If we place ourselves back under law, we give sin a power from which Jesus died to set us free. Grab ahold of that. Consider:

> For while we were in the flesh, the sinful passions, which were aroused by the Law [νόμος], were at work in the members of our body to bear fruit for death. 6 But now we have been released from the Law, having died to that by which we were bound, so that we serve in newness of the Spirit and not in oldness of the letter.
>
> Romans 7:5-6

Law arouses sin. We should abhor legalism. It is an affront to the Cross. NT laws do exist, but they are under the banner of Romans 8's Law of the Spirit of Life:

> Therefore there is now no condemnation for those who are in Christ Jesus. 2 For the law of the Spirit of life in Christ Jesus has set you free from the law of sin and of death. 3 For what the Law could not do, weak as it was through the flesh, God did: sending His own Son in the likeness of sinful flesh and as an offering for sin, He condemned sin in the flesh, 4 so that the requirement of the Law might be fulfilled in us, who do not walk according to the flesh but according to the Spirit.
>
> Romans 8:1-4

The answer to the lust of the flesh has never been law. For the Christians, neither has it been expulsion of a demon. The answer is to walk by the Spirit. To walk by the Spirit one must have a relationship with the Holy Spirit. You can't walk by the Spirit according to a set of rules. Rules and formulas don't work with Him. In fact, without the Holy Spirit's assistance even a Christian is powerless to obey the Word of God. Just try obeying the Sermon on the Mount without a deep relationship with the Holy Spirit.

We want easy answers, but learning to walk by the Spirit is difficult. Anyone who has fought to get the victory over a sinful habit knows what I mean. The truth is we must crucify the works of the flesh. The NT wording is strong: *For if you live according to the flesh you will die; but if by the Spirit you put to death the deeds of the body, you will live (Romans 8:13).* God holds us accountable for our conduct. He says put "put to death the deeds of the body." He does not say if you can't get victory it is because you have a demon living inside of you. That way of thinking is foreign to the fundamentals of the Bible. Even the legion of demons inside the man among the tombs could not keep that man from running to Jesus for help (Mark 5:6). Something to think about. Demons may be tempting you, for sure, but they cannot overrule you.

God deals with immaturity and blatant sin in different ways, though He does not condone or allow us to make excuses for sin. This truth is easily seen when looking into the life of King David: (...*because David did what was right in the sight of the LORD, and had not turned aside from anything that He commanded him all the days of his life, except in the case of Uriah the Hittite [1 Kings 15:5].*) Uncovering David's mistakes doesn't take much excavation. For example, David numbered Israel resulting in the angel killing 70,000 men (2 Samuel 24). But, God viewed that differently than how He judged David's murder of Uriah. Immaturity and mistakes are natural. They are viewed and dealt with by God quite differently than blatant sin. We absolutely have all we need to be victorious in this life. We have the Holy Spirit and God's word. And little by little we will, like the Israelites, possess our promised land. It is not because we are expelling demons out of our soul or body, but because we are working with and yielding to the Holy Spirit, learning to walk by the Spirit, and putting up a good fight. *His divine power has given to us all things that pertain to life and godliness, through the knowledge of Him who called us by glory and virtue (2 Peter 1:3).* I'm quite sure He is enough, and I'm in good company for that is exactly what the Lord said to Paul when he was dealing with Satan's thorn in his flesh (2 Corinthians 12).

God is totally into deliverance, but maybe differently than we think. In 1981 I was totally and instantly delivered from smoking two packs of cigarettes a day. Friends prayed for me and a prophetic word was spoken. God said He was delivering me and He did. Completely gone! Other things He hasn't made that easy. I know I have the ability to overcome all of them, because the Holy Spirit lives in me, however I have yet to apprehend what He's provided. I too need to crucify the works of the flesh.

We could end here, but the NT doesn't. It gives more instructions about what it is to walk by the Spirit apprehending victory.

Be Strong: Stand Firm

Ephesians 6 explains we can stand against the enemy in the evil day and how. It further describes some of the preparations necessary to be strong in the Lord and to stand. Alert: faith quenches *all* the fiery darts of the enemy:

> *Finally, be strong in the Lord and in the strength of His might. 11 Put on the full armor of God, so that you will be able to stand firm against the schemes of the devil. 12 For our struggle is not against flesh and blood, but against the rulers, against the powers, against the world forces of this darkness, against the spiritual forces of wickedness in the heavenly places. 13 Therefore, take up the full armor of God, so that you will be able to resist in the evil day, and having done everything, to stand firm. 14 Stand firm therefore, HAVING GIRDED YOUR LOINS WITH TRUTH, and HAVING PUT ON THE BREASTPLATE OF RIGHTEOUSNESS, 15 and having shod YOUR FEET WITH THE PREPARATION OF THE GOSPEL OF PEACE; 16 in addition to all, taking up the shield of faith with which you will be able to extinguish all the flaming arrows of the evil one. 17 And take THE HELMET OF SALVATION, and the sword of the Spirit, which is the word of God. 18 With all prayer and petition pray at all times in the Spirit, and with this in view, be on the alert with all perseverance and petition for all the saints.*
>
> *Ephesians 6:10-18*

Looking closely at Ephesians 6, clearly we see these scriptures are not dealing with demonic possession or invasion within a believer. Rather: *so that [we] will be able to stand firm against the schemes of the devil.* And, *so that [we] will be able to resist in the evil day, and having done everything, to stand firm (6:11).* Our ardent and resolute stance against the kingdom of darkness' assaults by the power of the Holy Spirit within us is essential. This can only be accomplished if we know who He is and who we are in

Him. Consider the casualties inflicted upon the Lord's camp when believers don't know who they are in Him. How many are still living in a works mentality? And yet, righteousness is one of the vital pieces of armor and repentance from dead works is foundational. Hebrews 5 says that we remain babies if we don't understand the teaching about righteousness (Hebrews 5:13). Babies do not advance against the kingdom of darkness. We must grow up knowing who we are in Him and He in us.

God, is that You?

Our problem may be God. Well, not really God, but, He may be behind our troubles. In reality, our problem is often in the mirror. Some of the problems people have that they think are attacks from a devil may actually be God resisting them. Sure, maybe it's an actual attack from the enemy, but God could be the instigator. He can and does, at times, allow a demon access to us for our own good (Paul's thorn in his flesh in 2 Corinthians 12). James and 1 Peter (both NT) deal with this very issue:

But He gives a greater grace. Therefore it says, "GOD IS OPPOSED TO THE PROUD, BUT GIVES GRACE TO THE HUMBLE." 7 Submit therefore to God. Resist the devil and he will flee from you. 8 Draw near to God and He will draw near to you. Cleanse your hands, you sinners; and purify your hearts, you double-minded. 9 Be miserable and mourn and weep; let your laughter be turned into mourning and your joy to gloom. 10 Humble yourselves in the presence of the Lord, and He will exalt you.

James 4:6-10

You younger men, likewise, be subject to your elders; and all of you, clothe yourselves with humility toward one another, for GOD IS OPPOSED TO THE PROUD, BUT GIVES GRACE TO THE HUMBLE. 6 Therefore humble yourselves under the mighty hand of God, that He may exalt you at the proper time, 7 casting all your anxiety on Him, because He cares for you. 8 Be of sober spirit, be on the alert. Your adversary, the devil, prowls around like a roaring lion, seeking someone to devour. 9 But resist him, firm in your faith, knowing that the same experiences of suffering are being accomplished by your brethren who are in the world. 10 After you have suffered for a little while, the God of all grace, who called you to His eternal glory in Christ, will Himself perfect, confirm, strengthen and establish you. 11 To Him be dominion forever and ever. Amen.

1 Peter 5:5-10

Working through these two sections of nearly identical scripture we find a problem, a cause, an effect, and a solution. Pride is the problem: a self-led life. Pride leads to an open door for attack from the enemy, allowed by God, in order that we will humble ourselves and repent. God uses the enemy as a tool in our lives. Just as He used Assyria and Babylon, enemies of Israel, to accomplish His purpose in the OT. Both nations were used by God, for a time, to discipline His people. Later God judged both nations. (This subject is discussed further in the next chapter, Truth in Tension.) What is the answer in both James and 1 Peter? Do they say to cast out a demon? No, both James and Peter say it begins with humility—submission to God. Submitting to God panics the devil.

The devil is described as a roaring lion seeking someone to devour. We have all likely been around household cats. They are fierce little hunters. Consider what that little kitty would be like as a 550 lbs. male lion charging at you at a speed of 50 mph! He hides in the tall grass waiting for an opportunity. He is hunting you. But there is a way to cause fear in him. Humbly submit to God. Then resist him firm in your faith. He will run from you, but probably only again to the tall grass—waiting and lurking. In Luke 4:13, after the temptation in the desert, we see that the devil left Jesus until a more opportune time. He knows if something works against us or not. As the devil watched Jesus he will watch us too. He will be back looking for an opportune time: a time when we are likely not expecting him. He will try to catch us off guard. To the Corinthians Paul issues this warning: *Therefore let him who thinks he stands take heed lest he fall (1 Corinthians 10:12).*

James concludes his section:

> *Draw near to God and He will draw near to you. Cleanse your hands, you sinners; and purify your hearts, you double-minded. 9 Be miserable and mourn and weep; let your laughter be turned into mourning and your joy to gloom. 10 Humble yourselves in the presence of the Lord, and He will exalt you.*
>
> James 4:8-10

It sounds harsh at face-value. But these are God's words. What's His point? Have suitable remorse for your sins. God is always drawing us near. He waits for a response from us.

Through all our suffering we must keep our eyes on Christ. Focusing on Him will both keep us from sin and also will aid us in victory over sin (Hebrews 12:2). Suffering brings a unique dynamic—a tremendous opportunity to lose heart and fall from steadfastness during the suffering. And, of course, the enemy is lurking; prowling; watching. We must win: stand our ground and possess our lentil field (2 Samuel 23:11-12).

Pride Leads to a Fall

> *A bishop then must be blameless... 6 not a novice, lest being puffed up with pride he fall into the same condemnation as the devil. 7 Moreover he must have a good testimony among those who are outside, lest he fall into reproach and the snare of the devil.*
>
> *1 Timothy 3:2, 3:6-7*

"Condemnation" in the Greek denotes judgment in a legal case. People need time to walk with God before they enter into leadership. Just because someone is a leader in society does not translate over to the Kingdom. Time allows us to learn how to conduct ourselves among the fellowship of believers and resist the enemies' traps. Pride is often a snare to leaders and will bring us behind God's woodshed. I doubt, dear reader, either of us want to go there.

Anyone who has served God for a while knows there are certain things about walking with Him we just don't learn any other way than simply walking with Him. We need time walking with and being with the Lord, learning His ways and character. There are levels of humility and death to self we just can't learn through textbook Christianity. It is a daily walk with the Holy Spirit that teaches us. Yes we must know His Word, but just knowing His Word won't give us what we need to endure everything coming our way. The Word and the Spirit together will. This is why God says not to ordain novices to leadership. Attacks will come and He wants us to be strong and win. Someone who has stood time after time will more likely have the character and endurance leaders need. If leaders fall, not only does their sin hurt them, but there is a ripple effect. Sin in God's people also exposes the Lord to open shame. Both Hebrews 6:6 and Romans 2:24 point this out, as does the story of David and Bathsheba. God said to King David in 2 Samuel 12:14: *"However, because by this deed you have given great occasion to the enemies of the LORD to blaspheme, the child also who is born to you shall surely die."* Sadly, we know the story; David sinned, God judged, and more than David and Bathsheba were touched by this tragedy.

Chapter 4

Truth in Tension

Truth in Tension is an apparent contradiction in scripture. Careful exegesis will find the gem of truth supporting the balance. Some things in scripture are hard to understand, as even Peter said of things Paul wrote (2 Peter 3). God granting the devil access to His children, or people in general, is one of those "hard to understand" things. He does it in His sovereignty with a purpose. In the heavenly realm, Satan saw the hedge of protection God had placed around Job. Satan needed God's permission to break through that hedge, gaining access to Job. Even then he had boundaries and was on a very tight leash in the hand of God. To gain access to Peter, Satan again had to ask God for permission. But what about all the "God's protection" and the "devil fleeing" scriptures? Can Satan or a demon have access to you or to me? That, dear reader, is the subject of this chapter—it is our truth in tension.

The following are three specific areas of scripture we will study to discover this truth in tension: 1 John 5:18, 2 Corinthians 12:7-10, and Luke 22:31-32. We will also look closely at the Greek Lexicon's definitions of the weightier words in each scripture.

The Wicked One DOES NOT Touch Him

We know that no one who is born of God sins; but He who was born of God keeps him, and the evil one does not touch him.

1 John 5:18

Greek Lexicon definitions:

Keeps τηρέω:
1) to attend to carefully, take care of
1a) to guard
1b) metaph. to keep, one in the state in which he is
1c) to observe
1d) to reserve: to undergo something

Touch ἅπτω:
1) to fasten to, adhere to
1a) to fasten fire to a thing, kindle, set of fire

A Thorn in the Flesh

Because of the surpassing greatness of the revelations, for this reason, to keep me from exalting myself, there was given me a thorn in the flesh, a messenger of Satan to torment me—to keep me from exalting myself! 8 Concerning this I implored the Lord three times that it might leave me. 9 And He has said to me, "My grace is sufficient for you, for power is perfected in weakness." Most gladly, therefore, I will rather boast about my weaknesses, so that the power of Christ may dwell in me. 10 Therefore I am well content with weaknesses, with insults, with distresses, with persecutions, with difficulties, for Christ's sake; for when I am weak, then I am strong.

2 Corinthians 12:7-10

Greek Lexicon definitions:

Thorn σκόλοψ: (this word only occurs once in the NT)
1) a pointed piece of wood, a pale, a stake
2) a sharp stake, splinter

Flesh σάρξ:
1) flesh (the soft substance of the living body, which covers the bones and is permeated with blood) of both man and beasts
2) the body
   2a) the body of a man
   2b) used of natural or physical origin, generation or relationship
      2b1) born of natural generation
   2c) the sensuous nature of man, "the animal nature"
      2c1) without any suggestion of depravity
      2c2) the animal nature with cravings which incite to sin
      2c3) the physical nature of man as subject to suffering

3) a living creature (because possessed of a body of flesh) whether man or beast

4) the flesh, denotes mere human nature, the earthly nature of man apart from divine influence, and therefore prone to sin and opposed to God

Messenger ἄγγελος:
   1) a messenger, envoy, one who is sent
   2) an angel … (2f is the only definition that applies)
      2f) some angels have proven faithless to the trust committed to them by God, and have given themselves over to sin and now obey the devil

Torment κολαφίζω:
   1) to strike with the fist, give one a blow with the fist
   2) to maltreat, treat with violence and contumely

Sifting Peter

"Simon, Simon, behold, Satan has demanded permission to sift you like wheat; 32 but I have prayed for you, that your faith may not fail; and you, when once you have turned again, strengthen your brothers."

Luke 22:31-32

Greek Lexicon definitions:
   Sift σινιάζω:
      1) to sift, shake in a sieve
      2) fig. by inward agitation to try one's faith to the verge of overthrow

   Turned ἐπιστρέφω :
      1) transitively
      1a) to turn to
      1a1) to the worship of the true God
      1b) to cause to return, to bring back
      1b1) to the love and obedience of God
      1b2) to the love for the children
      1b3) to love wisdom and righteousness
      2) intransitively
      2a) to turn to one's self
      2b) to turn one's self about, turn back
      2c) to return, turn back, come back

Tension

From 1 John 5:18 we understand if one keeps himself then the wicked one can't touch him. Also, James 4:6-7 says: *But He gives a greater grace. Therefore it says, "GOD IS OPPOSED TO THE PROUD, BUT GIVES GRACE TO THE HUMBLE." 7 Submit therefore to God. Resist the devil and he will flee from you.*

Remember that 1 John 5:18 and James 4:6-7 are both written to the Christian. Furthermore, no one can submit to God unless they are born of His Spirit. But, what if a Christian doesn't keep himself, doesn't live humbly, and doesn't submit to God, and resist the devil? Does this give the devil a license to touch, adhere to, cling to, or fasten to that Christian? Does this mean we have to be perfect in order to keep our self? Philippians 3 brings light to this subject. In Philippians 3:12-14 we see the heart of God concerning perfection verses walking where we have attained. Though Paul had not yet apprehended what he was aiming for, he walked where he had attained. David, as we discussed earlier, only sinned concerning Uriah, though David made many mistakes (1 Kings 15:5). Hebrews 10:38 also says: *"BUT MY RIGHTEOUS ONE SHALL LIVE BY FAITH; AND IF HE SHRINKS BACK, MY SOUL HAS NO PLEASURE IN HIM."*

These scriptures are just a few among the many that allow us to safely know that it is not a matter of our perfection. Rather, it is a matter of walking where we've attained and when we stumble, returning. God will protect us no matter how immature we are. One of the Holy Spirit's ministries is to keep us moving closer to the character of Christ. He will also discipline us if we start going astray. That is a function of His grace and love towards us, revealing His commitment to make us like His Son. In this He reveals His devotion to complete what He has begun in us. Our responsibility is to be found in Him, doing our best to rely on His grace, not trusting our own righteousness, and walking where we've attained. And we are to have faith in God and His protection. Faith is our spiritual vital signs. As goes our faith, so goes our walk. By faith we are saved. By faith we apprehend the promises of God. By faith we quench *all* the fiery darts of the evil one.

If we begin to backslide, start getting puffed up in pride, stop seeking Him, stop trusting Him, or start to rely on our self, and our deeds instead of Jesus' righteousness, then God will begin to oppose us. What does this mean to be opposed by God? Opposed means (GL): 1) to range in battle against 2) to oppose one's self, resist. So, God will battle against, oppose Himself against and resist the proud—even if that proud person is a Christian. What subsequent action does God take to bring the Christian back to Himself and into humble submission?

Hebrews 12 explains the discipline of God. Hebrews 12 says that if God loves us He will disciple us. God has His many tools to use behind the spiritual woodshed. One of which can be the devil. Yes, in the life of a believer, the devil can be a tool in the hand of God. Two NT examples of this are found in Paul's thorn in his flesh and the sifting Peter went through during the time leading up to and during the crucifixion. And likely up to the time Jesus met them on the shore in John 21.

First let's look at Paul's thorn in the flesh. A question must be asked, who gave Paul the thorn? What we know:

1. the thorn was in his flesh;
2. it was a messenger of Satan;
3. it was meant to keep him humble.

Paul says the thorn in his flesh was due to his abundant revelations. Its source must have been God, since the messenger was mean to keep Paul humble. Remember God resists the proud, but gives grace to the humble. Satan would want Paul proud. He wouldn't give him something, by choice, to keep him humble. It therefore appears the enemy was clueless about God using him to keep Paul humble. Satan saw access to Paul and took it without understanding it was meant to make Paul more like Jesus.

The thorn was in his flesh. (Note that Paul uses an entirely different word in verses 2-3 for "body.") This word "flesh" is the same word used in Romans 7:18: *For I know that nothing good dwells in me, that is, in my flesh…* The thorn was not in his soul or spirit, but in his flesh. The messenger was allowed to torment (NKJV: buffet) Paul. Torment means (GL), "to strike with the fist; origin from: kolaphos (a blow with the fist)." For example when someone hits you, the blow came from the outside and was felt on the inside, as well. Was the punch from the inside? No, it came from the outside, but was felt inside too. Though external, the punch effected the internal. Naturally, when you receive a blow to your body there is internal bleeding resulting in a bruise. This thorn was allowed by God, because Paul would be better off with it than without it. The purpose of the thorn, though it was a messenger of Satan, was to keep Paul's character in check. Thus, the Lord uses the devil much like a sheep dog—to keep the sheep reigned in. The messenger of Satan was only a tool in the hand of God, used for the benefit of the child of God.

Jesus told Peter that Satan had asked permission to sift him. Jesus implies He gave Satan permission, since Jesus then says that He prayed for Peter that his faith wouldn't fail. Jesus then prophesies to Peter: he would deny Jesus that very day and then the rooster would crow. Note that the devil *asked* permission. Satan had to go through God for permission before he could get to Peter. Remarkable!

Allow me to paraphrase. "Simon, Satan has asked and I have given him access to you. It will be a hard time for you, in fact you will even disown Me three times. After you deny Me the third time, a rooster will crow. When this happens, remember I already knew it would happen. It doesn't change the fact that I love you. I know that all will desert Me; it must happen to fulfill all the prophecies. Peter, it will be a dark time for you, but in the end, when the sifting is over, you will be stronger. Peter, when you return to Me, go strengthen your brothers. I will use this for good! The devil intends it for evil, but he is only a tool in My hand. I will use him to accomplish My purpose. I prayed for you, Peter. Your faith will not fail." The rooster crowed, Jesus turned—their eyes met. Can you imagine how Peter felt?

God's use of our enemies to accomplish His purposes and plans can be found throughout the entirety of the Bible: Genesis through Revelation. Even Jesus' betrayal by Judas is an example. Judas' betrayal was prophesied in the OT. The prophecy stated that Jesus would be betrayed for a price of 30 pieces of silver (Jeremiah 32:6-9 and Matthew 27:3-10).

The devil was used to fulfill prophecy by inciting Judas! Another example is the woman with the infirmity. Luke 13:16 states her condition was brought on by Satan. Yet it was also the very thing that drove her to Jesus for healing. God using the devil to accomplish His purpose through the Cross is the ultimate!

To summarize: Can the devil touch us? No, if we are walking with God. Yes, if we aren't. Also, yes, if God allows it for our benefit. Though he must ask permission. And even then he is on a short leash and is under constant surveillance by God.

Chapter 5

Liars

W E ARE AT WAR WITH THE DEVIL and his evil spirits. They are liars and deceivers and they want to destroy us. Beings whose desire is to be worshipped; the devil lusts for the devotion and heights belonging only to God (Isaiah 14 and Ezekiel 28). Evil spirits will do anything they can to lead us astray. God demands that we are Christ centered and kingdom focused. He commands us to love Him first and entirely. Satan hungers for attention and devotion. And he is not passive about it. Talking about him attracts and invites him. He is a narcissist and doesn't deserve the attention he craves. Many Christians are demon focused, don't be. If we encounter a demon—deal with it, but don't go hunting.

Some Christians rely on personal experiences to persuade others that demons can live inside Christians. Their conclusions, forming their theology, are based on observations and experiences with demons. If demons can scream while coming out of someone, can't they scream while not coming out of someone? They are liars; they are deceivers. It is dangerous [understatement] to build doctrine on their activity. Our theology must not be experience based, it must be Bible based. We must build upon the foundational truth of the Bible. We then evaluate our experiences according to what it says.

Here is my personal experience with a lying spirit. A person my husband and I had known for years came by for a visit one night. We'd had many discussions over the years with this friend about demons and their activity and authority in a believer's life. Their theology was that demons can be inside Christians. They also taught others according to their views. This person also had influence with many people. They knew both my husband and I disagreed with them regarding demons dwelling inside Christians. This night in particular they were more aggressive than usual. After 30 minutes or so, discussing demons and their activity, I had a spirit grab my throat and I heard a voice demand with great assertion that I let it out. I felt an intense urgency and compulsion to do what it insisted— no, demanded! Instead, I did nothing. I was perplexed at the experience.

What had happened? I asked God for understanding, since I believed, and still do believe, the Bible teaches that the Holy Spirit does not allow demons inside of Christians. Later, I discussed my experience with my husband. He immediately responded with, "Oh, so demons hang around [our friend] to promote their doctrine. Hum!"

Immediately I understood the demon was trying to persuade me that he was inside of me. And since he was inside of me, I needed to get him out. This of course was a lie, but then what can we expect from a demon? I'm sure if had I had given into its lie and tried to "get it out" the demon would have manifested in support of its lie, though I'm only speculating. Our friend was promoting a doctrine of demons and demons were hanging around to help them promote it. They were, in fact, giving place to the devil.

If the demon had really been inside me, would it have demanded I let it out? The Bible teaches demons want instead to inhabit people. So why did this one demand I let it out? It was all a big lie. The demon wanted to convince me, through experience, it was in me. It wanted me to believe its lie. I wonder how many so-called "deliverance" sessions are nothing more than lying deceiving spirits promoting their doctrines to those who will believe them.

If I had built my theology based upon my experience, instead of what I knew to be true in the Bible, my conclusions would have been different. I would have a theology based upon demons and their activity. A doctrine of demons. The Bible is objective; our experiences are subjective. We must build our doctrines based upon what God says in the Bible. We then evaluate our experiences accordingly.

Now to Him who is able to keep you from stumbling,
And to present you faultless
Before the presence of His glory with exceeding joy,
To God our Savior, Who alone is wise,
Be glory and majesty, Dominion and power,
Both now and forever.
Amen.
Jude 24-25

The Finale

Grace and peace be multiplied to you in the knowledge of God and of Jesus our Lord, 3 as His divine power has given to us all things that pertain to life and godliness, through the knowledge of Him who called us by glory and virtue, 4 by which have been given to us exceedingly great and precious promises, that through these you may be partakers of the divine nature, having escaped the corruption that is in the world through lust.

5 But also for this very reason, giving all diligence, add to your faith virtue, to virtue knowledge, 6 to knowledge self-control, to self-control perseverance, to perseverance godliness, 7 to godliness brotherly kindness, and to brotherly kindness love. 8 For if these things are yours and abound, you will be neither barren nor unfruitful in the knowledge of our Lord Jesus Christ. 9 For he who lacks these things is shortsighted, even to blindness, and has forgotten that he was cleansed from his old sins. 10 Therefore, brethren, be even more diligent to make your call and election sure, for if you do these things you will never stumble; 11 for so an entrance will be supplied to you abundantly into the everlasting kingdom of our Lord and Savior Jesus Christ.

12 For this reason I will not be negligent to remind you always of these things, though you know and are established in the present truth.

2 Peter 1:2-11

Appendix

Definitions for curse, cursing, and cursed from the Online Bible Greek Lexicon.

Old Testament

1. 07043 קלל qalal kaw-lal'

Genesis 8:21 *The LORD smelled the soothing aroma; and the LORD said to Himself, "I will never again curse <07043> the ground on account of man, for the intent of man's heart is evil from his youth; and I will never again destroy every living thing, as I have done."*
a primitive root; v; [BDB-886a] {See TWOT on 2028 }
AV-curse 39, swifter 5, light thing 5, vile 4, lighter 4, despise 3, abated 2, ease 2, light 2, lighten 2, slightly 2, misc 12; 82
1) to be slight, be swift, be trifling, be of little account, be light
1a) (Qal)
1a1) to be slight, be abated (of water)
1a2) to be swift
1a3) to be trifling, be of little account
1b) (Niphal)
1b1) to be swift, show oneself swift
1b2) to appear trifling, be too trifling, be insignificant
1b3) to be lightly esteemed
1c) (Piel)
1c1) to make despicable
1c2) to curse
1d) (Pual) to be cursed
1e) (Hiphil)
1e1) to make light, lighten
1e2) to treat with contempt, bring contempt or dishonour
1f) (Pilpel)
1f1) to shake

1f2) to whet

1g) (Hithpalpel) to shake oneself, be moved to and fro

2. 0779 ארר 'arar aw-rar'

Genesis 12:3 *"And I [God] will bless those who bless you [Abraham], And the one who curses <07043> you I will curse <0779>. And in you all the families of the earth will be blessed."*
a primitive root; v; [BDB-76b] {See TWOT on 168 }
AV-curse 62, bitterly 1; 63
1) to curse
1a) (Qal)
1a1) to curse
1a2) cursed be he (participle used as in curses)
1b) (Niphal) to be cursed, cursed
1c) (Piel) to curse, lay under a curse, put a curse on
1d) (Hophal) to be made a curse, be cursed

3. 01288 ברך barak baw-rak' (used in conjunction with <03808> "no, not" to render the translation "curse."

1 Kings 21:9-10 *Now she [Jezebal] wrote in the letters, saying, "Proclaim a fast and seat Naboth at the head of the people; 10 and seat two worthless men before him, and let them testify against him, saying, 'You cursed <01288> God and the king.' Then take him out and stone him to death."*
a primitive root; v; [BDB-138b] {See TWOT on 285 }
AV-bless 302, salute 5, curse 4, blaspheme 2, blessing 2, praised 2, kneel down 2, congratulate 1, kneel 1, make to kneel 1, misc 8; 330
1) to bless, kneel
1a) (Qal)
1a1) to kneel
1a2) to bless
1b) (Niphal) to be blessed, bless oneself
1c) (Piel) to bless
1d) (Pual) to be blessed, be adored
1e) (Hiphil) to cause to kneel
1f) (Hithpael) to bless oneself

2) (TWOT) to praise, salute, curse

4. 06895 קבב qabab kaw-bab'

Numbers 23:8 *"How shall I curse <06895> whom God has not cursed <06895>? And how can I denounce whom the LORD has not denounced?"*
a primitive root; v; [BDB-866b] {See TWOT on 1978 }
AV-curse 7, at all 1; 8
1) to curse, utter a curse against
1a) (Qal) to curse

5. 02194 זעם za'am zaw-am'

Proverbs 22:14 *The mouth of an adulteress is a deep pit; He who is cursed <02194> of the LORD will fall into it.*
a primitive root; v; [BDB-276b] {See TWOT on 568 }
AV-indignation 4, defy 3, abhor 2, angry 2, abominable 1; 12
1) to denounce, express indignation, be indignant
1a) (Qal)
1a1) to have indignation, be indignant, be angrily indignant, be defiant
1a2) to be abhorrent
1a3) to express indignation in speech, denounce, curse
1b) (Niphal) to show indignation, show anger

6. 07045 קללה qᵉlalah kel-aw-law'

Genesis 27:12 *"Perhaps my father [Isaac] will feel me [Jacob], then I will be as a deceiver in his sight, and I will bring upon myself a curse <07045> and not a blessing."*
from 07043; n f; [BDB-887a] {See TWOT on 2028 @@ "2028d" }
AV-curse 27, cursing 5, accursed 1; 33
1) curse, vilification, execration

7. 0423 אלה 'alah aw-law'

Numbers 5:21 *(then the priest shall have the woman swear with the oath of the curse, and the priest shall say to the woman),* "the LORD make you a curse <0423>

and an oath among your people by the LORD'S *making your thigh waste away and your abdomen swell."*
from 0422; n f; [BDB-46b] {See TWOT on 91 @@ "91a" }
AV-curse 18, oath 14, execration 2, swearing 2; 36
1) oath
2) oath of covenant
3) curse
3a) from God
3b) from men
4) execration

8. 0422 אלה 'alah aw-law'

Judges 17:2 *He said to his mother, "The eleven hundred pieces of silver which were taken from you, about which you uttered a curse <0422> in my hearing, behold, the silver is with me; I took it." And his mother said, "Blessed be my son by the* LORD."
a primitive root; v; [BDB-46b] {See TWOT on 94 }
AV-swear 4, curse 1, adjure 1; 6
1) to swear, curse
1a) (Qal)
1a1) to swear, take an oath (before God)
1a2) to curse
1b) (Hiphil)
1b1) to put under oath, adjure
1b2) to put under a curse

9. 07650 שבע shaba' shaw-bah'

Psalm 102:8 *My enemies have reproached me all day long; Those who deride me have used my name as a curse <07650>.*
a primitive root; v; [BDB-989a] {See TWOT on 2319 }
AV-sware 167, charge 8, oath 7, adjure 3, straitly 2; 187
1) to swear, adjure
1a) (Qal) sworn (participle)
1b) (Niphal)
1b1) to swear, take an oath

1b2) to swear (of Jehovah by Himself)
1b3) to curse
1c) (Hiphil)
1c1) to cause to take an oath
1c2) to adjure

10. 03994 מארה mᵉerah meh-ay-raw'

Proverbs 3:33 *The curse <03994> of the LORD is on the house of the wicked, But He blesses the dwelling of the righteous.*
from 0779; n f; [BDB-76b] {See TWOT on 168 @@ "168a"}
AV-curse 4, cursing 1; 5
1) curse

11. 07621 שבועה shᵉbuw'ah sheb-oo-aw'

Isaiah 65:15 *"You will leave your name for a curse to My chosen ones, And the Lord GOD will slay you. But <07621> My servants will be called by another name."*
pass part of 07650; n f; [BDB-989b] {See TWOT on 2319 @@ "2319a"}
AV-oath 28, sworn + 01167 1, curse 1; 30
1) oath, curse
1a) oath
1a1) attesting of innocence
1a2) curse
1b) oath (of Jehovah)

12. 08381 תאלה ta'alah tah-al-aw'

Lamentations 3:65 *You will give them hardness of heart, Your curse <08381> will be on them.*
from 0422; n f; [BDB-46b] {See TWOT on 94 @@ "94b"}
AV-curse 1; 1
1) curse

13. 02764 חרם cherem khay'-rem or (#Zec 14:11) חרם cherem kheh'-rem

Malachi 4:5-6 *"Behold, I am going to send you Elijah the prophet before the coming of the great and terrible day of the LORD. 6 He will restore the hearts of the fathers to their children and the hearts of the children to their fathers, so that I will not come and smite the land with a curse <02764>."*
from 02763; n m; [BDB-356a, BDB-357a] {See TWOT on 744 @@ "744a" }
{See TWOT on 745 @@ "745a" }
AV-net 9, accursed thing 9, accursed 4, curse 4, cursed thing 3, devoted 3, destruction 2, devoted thing 2, dedicated thing 1, destroyed 1; 38
1) a thing devoted, thing dedicated, ban, devotion
2) a net, thing perforated
3) have been utterly destroyed, (appointed to) utter destruction

New Testament

14. 2671 κατάρα katara kat-ar'-ah

Galatians 3:10 *For as many as are of the works of the Law are under a curse <2671>; for it is written, "CURSED <1944> IS EVERYONE WHO DOES NOT ABIDE BY ALL THINGS WRITTEN IN THE BOOK OF THE LAW, TO PERFORM THEM."*
from 2596 (intensive) and 685; n f; TDNT-1:449,75; {See TDNT 90 }
AV-curse 3, cursing 2, cursed 1; 6
1) an execration, imprecation, curse

15. 2672 καταράομαι kataraomai kat-ar-ah'-om-ahee

Mark 11:21 *Being reminded, Peter said to Him, "Rabbi, look, the fig tree which You cursed <2672> has withered."*
middle voice from 2671; v; TDNT-1:448,75; {See TDNT 90 }
AV-curse 6; 6
1) to curse, doom, imprecate evil upon

16. 1944 ἐπικατάρατος epikataratos ep-ee-kat-ar'-at-os

Galatians 3:13-14 *Christ redeemed us from the curse of the Law, having become a curse for us — for it is written, "CURSED <1944> IS EVERYONE WHO HANGS ON A TREE" — 14 in order that in Christ Jesus the blessing of Abraham might come to the Gentiles, so that we would receive the promise of the Spirit through faith.*

from 1909 and a derivative of 2672; adj; TDNT-1:451,75; { See TDNT 90 }
AV-cursed 3; 3
1) accursed, execrable, exposed to divine vengeance, lying under God's curse

17. 332 ἀναθεματίζω anathematizo an-ath-em-at-id'-zo

Acts 23:21 *"So do not listen to them, for more than forty of them are lying in wait for him who have bound themselves under a curse <332> not to eat or drink until they slay him; and now they are ready and waiting for the promise from you."*
from 331; v; TDNT-1:355,57; {See TDNT 65 }
AV-curse 1, bind under a curse 1, bind with an oath 1, bind under a great curse + 331 1; 4
1) to devote to destruction
2) to declare one's self liable to the severest divine penalties

18. 2617 καταισχύνω kataischuno kat-ahee-skhoo'-no

Matthew 26:74 *Then he began to curse <2617> and swear, "I do not know the man!" And immediately a rooster crowed.*
from 2596 and 153; v; TDNT-1:189,29; {See TDNT 37 }
AV-ashamed 7, confound 3, dishonour 2, shame 1; 13
1) to dishonour, disgrace
2) to put to shame, make ashamed
2a) to be ashamed, blush with shame
2b) one is said to be put to shame who suffers a repulse, or whom some hope has deceived

19. 2616 καταδυναστεύω katadunasteuo kat-ad-oo-nas-tyoo'-o
Revelation 22:3 *There will no longer be any curse <2616>; and the throne of God and of the Lamb will be in it, and His bond-servants will serve Him.*
from 2596 and a derivative of 1413; v;
AV-oppress 2; 2
1) to exercise harsh control over one, to use one's power against one
2) to oppress one

20. 685 ἀρά ara ar-ah'

Romans 3:14 *"WHOSE MOUTH IS FULL OF CURSING <685> AND BITTERNESS."*
probably from 142; n f; TDNT-1:448,75; {See TDNT 90 }
AV-cursing 1; 1
1) a prayer, a supplication
2) an imprecation, curse, malediction

Made in the USA
Columbia, SC
19 February 2019